# Poland Between the Superpowers

# Westview Replica Editions

The concept of Westview Replica Editions is a response to the continuing crisis in academic and informational publishing. Library budgets for books have been severely curtailed. Ever larger portions of general library budgets are being diverted from the purchase of books and used for data banks, computers, micromedia, and other methods of information retrieval. Inter-library loan structures further reduce the edition sizes required to satisfy the needs of the scholarly community. Economic pressures on the university presses and the few private scholarly publishing companies have severely limited the capacity of the industry to properly serve the academic and research communities. As a result, many manuscripts dealing with important subjects, often representing the highest level of scholarship, are no longer economically viable publishing projects--or, if accepted for publication, are typically subject to lead times ranging from one to three years.

Westview Replica Editions are our practical solution to the problem. We accept a manuscript in camera-ready form, typed according to our specifications, and move it immediately into the production process. As always, the selection criteria include the importance of the subject, the work's contribution to scholarship, and its insight, originality of thought, and excellence of exposition. The responsibility for editing and proofreading lies with the author or sponsoring institution. We prepare chapter headings and display pages, file for copyright, and obtain Library of Congress Cataloging in Publication Data. A detailed manual contains simple instructions for preparing the final typescript, and our editorial staff is always available to answer questions.

The end result is a book printed on acid-free paper and bound in sturdy library-quality soft covers. We manufacture these books ourselves using equipment that does not require a lengthy make-ready process and that allows us to publish first editions of 300 to 600 copies and to reprint even smaller quantities as needed. Thus, we can produce Replica Editions quickly and can keep even very specialized books in print as long as there is a demand for them.

# About the Book and Author

*Poland Between the Superpowers:*
*Security vs. Economic Recovery*
Arthur R. Rachwald

This book examines the foreign and domestic policies of Poland
since World War II in light of the country's relations with the
Soviet Union and the United States. Dr. Rachwald focuses on three
salient goals of Polish foreign policy: security, guaranteed both
by alliance with the Soviet Union and by support for the idea of
European collective security; territorial integrity, evidenced by
Poland's effort to obtain unconditional, international recognition
of its western border (the Oder-Neisse line) as the final legal
frontier between Poland and the German states; and domestic political stability and economic contacts with the West. Dr. Rachwald
argues that these goals have frequently been mutually exclusive and
unequally pursued; whenever the leaders of Poland have been presented with a choice between security and prosperity, they have
chosen security as the primary aim of foreign policy.

Dr. Rachwald is assistant professor of political science at
the United States Naval Academy.

To Anna

# Poland Between the Superpowers

## Security vs. Economic Recovery

Arthur R. Rachwald

Westview Press / Boulder, Colorado

*A Westview Replica Edition*

Published in 1983 in the United States of America by
    Westview Press, Inc.
    5500 Central Avenue
    Boulder, Colorado 80301
    Frederick A. Praeger, President and Publisher

Library of Congress Cataloging in Publication Data
Rachwald, Arthur R.
    Poland between the superpowers.

    (A Westview  replica edition)
    1. Poland--Foreign relations--1945-    . 2. Poland
--Politics and government--1945-1980.  3. Poland--
Politics and government--1980-    . I. Title.
DK4436.R3  1983      327.438        83-6758
ISBN 0-86531-975-8

Printed and bound in the United States of America.

10 9 8 7 6 5 4 3 2 1

# Contents

# Acknowledgment

I would like to express my special thanks to Ms. Sandra Erb for her care and patience in preparing this manuscript for publication.

# Introduction

Links between the international environment and domestic policies permeate the histories of all nations, but this interdependence appears particularly strong in the history of Poland. The country is a transition state where several political and cultural currents intersect. The area inhabited by the Polish people, the plains located between the Baltic Sea in the north and the Carpathian mountains in the south, provides a wide corridor between two distinct segments of Europe, and opens Poland to strong influence from both sides. Poland has natural borders in neither the east nor the west, and for security must rely on her own military strength and the support of her allies. This openness on two sides has involved Poland in relationships with nations so distant as France, the Mongolian Empire, Sweden and Turkey.

The cultural development of Poland has been shaped by the Christian ideas channeled by the Roman Catholic church. The church has molded the Polish nation according to the Western patterns transmitted for a thousand years to all layers of the society. Poland has experienced all major cultural and political trends of Western Europe, including the Renaissance, Reformation, Enlightenment, Romanticism and Positivism, constitutionalism and democracy. The popularization of these models, however, was frequently delayed for several decades, and their substance adjusted to compromise for the Slavic origin of the Poles and the influence from the East. Poland, in consequence, belongs to the peripheries of Western civilization.

The independent Polish state emerged in the second half of the tenth century, and its first choice was between East and West, that is, between the eastern or western form of Christianity. The decision to incorporate Poland into the Western world was a result of proximity to the Holy Roman Empire, and in 966, the Piast dynasty received baptism according to the Roman rite. Poland became the Christiana republica, and was placed under the pontifical protection of the Apostolic Sea.

xi

The conversion was a political step to establish ideological harmony between Poland and her powerful neighbor in the west. The essentially Teutonic Holy Roman Empire dominated the political sense of Poland. With few exceptions, the nation was unable to match Germany and had to accept sovereignty of the Empire. The country was also weakened by internal fragmentation into rival principalities, which facilitated German conquest and colonization. This process culminated in 1266, when the German Order of St. Mary, the Teutonic Knights, were invited to settle near the mouth of the Vistula. When in the fourteenth century Poland became united again, the country lost half of its original territory, including access to the Baltic Sea.

The second stage of Polish history was initiated with the conclusion of the Polish-Lithuanian union in 1386. This alliance strengthened the Polish state while Kievan Russia was conquered by the Mongols, the Holy Empire fragmented, and in 1410 the Teutonic Order was defeated by the united Polish-Lithuanian forces. Thus emerged the Jagiellonian Poland, expanding "from sea to sea," that is, from Baltic to the Black Sea.

The Commonwealth dominated over its international environment, but committed several diplomatic blunders. The "Prussian homage" allowed the Teutonic Order to survive as a secular state subordinated to Poland; the Poles consented to the succession of Habsburgs to the Bohemian and Hungarian thrones; neglected opportunities to check revival of Russia; and for centuries fought politically unnecessary religious wars with Turkey.

Poland's domestic system was one of democracy limited to the gentry. Formally instituted in 1348, it worked well for three centuries until its degeneration into the oligarchy of a few powerful magnates. Internal decay was also promoted by exhaustion from protracted wars with Sweden. At the same time, Prussia emancipated itself from Polish control, and the Grand Duchy of Moscow prepared the ground for the "gathering of the Russian land" crusade.

By the eighteenth century, Poland ceased to play an active role in Europe. The impoverished gentry fell under the economic and political control of the magnates manipulated by Poland's imperial neighbors, Russia in particular. This influence of backward agrarian states halted development of bourgeoisie, a new middle class capable of pulling Poland out of its domestic crisis. The foreign powers successfully frustrated numerous programs of socio-economic reform, and when in 1791 the nation succeeded in adopting a liberal constitution, it was promptly erased from the map of Europe.

Poland was partitioned (1772, 1793, 1795) by Russia, Prussia and Austria when the nation was recovering from lethargy. The loss of statehood triggered passionate patriotism and revolutionary enthusiasm. Independence became the sacred goal to be achieved by an altruistic policy of struggling for "your freedom and ours." For more than a century, the Poles were fighting foreign wars, especially for France and Britain, but without reciprocity.

Despite enormous Polish contribution on the French side, Napoleon created only the dwarfish Duchy of Warsaw, instead of supporting the idea of Poland within 1772 borders. This tiny state was even further reduced at the Congress of Vienna in 1815, renamed the Kingdom of Poland, and placed under Russian rule. It managed, however, to retain its liberal tradition, self-rule and army. Hated by the autocratic Russia, in 1830 the Polish army was ordered to suppress revolutions in Belgium and France. It was a provocation designed to facilitate Russian occupation of Poland. The Poles revolted, but, left without outside help, lost the war with Russia.

Following the uprising, the idea was born that Poland would never regain independence without the prior destruction of the Holy Alliance, the Congress of Vienna system in Europe. For the rest of the eighteenth century, the Poles fought on every revolutionary barricade in Europe. The revolutionary spirit inspired also the second major uprising against still feudal Russia. It erupted in January of 1863, ending in defeat and incorporation of Poland as "by-Vistula land" into the Russian Empire. Until World War I, Poland was subjected to intensive Germanization and Russification, confiscation of the Polish estates and mass exile to Siberia. To everyone's surprise, especially Lenin's, foreign domination only intensified Polish patriotism.

The outbreak of World War I was welcomed as an opportunity to liberate and reunite Poland. The simultaneous defeat of Germany and Russia gave Poland a realistic chance for independence, and as a French ally, Poland entered the Treaty of Versailles system of security aimed to contain Russia and Germany. But before Poland's independence became secured, the young republic had to drive back the invading Russian armies, which in the name of World Revolution were exporting Leninism to Germany. According to Lenin's plan, Poland was to be a component of the Soviet state.

The victory of 1920 established Poland's right to exist as an independent state. It was a very important victory, with all consequences becoming evident during World War II, when Soviet Russia reversed territorial results of the 1920 war, but respected Poland's claim to separate state.

In twenty years, the independent Poland was destroyed together with the Versailles Europe. Left without American support, France and her East European allies were unable to contain the resurgence of German and Russian nationalism when the two biggest nations in Europe committed to undo the results of World War I. In German view, Poland was only a sessional state whose existence was bound to an humiliating international system in Europe, and before getting at each other's throats, Nazi Germany and Soviet Russia partitioned Poland again in September of 1939.

Since the end of World War II Poland has been under Soviet domination of both her domestic and foreign policies. Like other Warsaw Pact nations, Poland must be governed by pro-Soviet communist party and follow Soviet line in all basic national

security matters.  These are two essential guarantees for the
preservation of the status quo in Europe.

But the Soviets are aware of the limits to their power.
Despite the official adherence to Marxism-Leninism, nationalism
of East European nations has prevailed over this foreign
ideology.  This development has found its expression in
reluctant Soviet endorsement of the national road to socialism
idea.  Also, the Soviets are incapable of administering the
every day affairs of their clients and have substantially
reduced the degree of their economic control.  Although still
dependent upon Moscow, the entire region has supplemented
economic ties to the USSR by developing extensive and lasting
relations with the West.

The case of Poland is of special importance.  In the first
place, the territorial composition and political system of
Poland was a highly controversial issue during the Second World
War becoming one of the main causes of the Cold War.  Secondly,
Poland and the German Democratic Republic, occupy a special
place in Europe owning to the location in the center of a
strategic corridor between East and West.  Finally, Poland
continues to be a very sensitive part of the Soviet empire
because of an intense anti-Russian and anti-Soviet nationalism,
a Western cultural tradition and political heritage of democracy
colored by anarchistic overtones.

However, Poland's experience during World War II
necessitated a reexamination of Polish political attitude toward
Russia leading to a limited convergence of the Polish and Soviet
security interest.  Poland evolved to become unorthodox but a
reliable international partner of the USSR, and the great
majority of Poles, regardless of their ideological orientations,
recognized the absolute priority of peaceful coexistence with
the powerful neighbor.

The examination of the foreign and domestic policies of
Poland has been organized in terms of policy goals.(1)  It is
the basic assumption of this study that Poland's salient
international objectives have been:

1.  security through alliance with the Soviet
    Union and support to the idea of the
    collective security in Europe as an
    alternative to the bloc politics;

2.  de jure recognition of the Oder-Neisse
    line as a final and permanent border
    between Poland and German states;

3.  political and economic recovery to assure
    stability at home and prestige abroad.

(1)  This approach has been developed by Wolfram F. Hanrieder,
West German Foreign Policy, 1949-1963 (Stanford, California:
Stanford University Press, 1967), Introduction.

*Arthur R. Rachwald*

# 1
# Security

## Alliance with the West

Poland's view of its historical mission was formed during the four hundred years of its coalition with Lithuania, a golden age that ended with the partitions of the late Eighteenth Century and the loss of Polish statehood. This was the heroic period when the Teutonic German Order, Ottoman Turkey, Protestant Sweden and Orthodox Russia were kept at bay by a multinational Polish commonwealth of nations stretching as a barrier from the Baltic to the Black Sea. It inspired a messianic concept of Polish foreign policy as a "bulwark of Christianity," and encouraged the belief that the countries of Western Europe, Catholic France and Italy, in particular, were Poland's natural allies and that their security depended directly on Poland's ability to shield Western civilization from Asian intruders and to balance Germany's power from the East.

Subjected to the arbitrary rule of the semi-feudal regimes of Prussia, Austria and Russia after the partitions, the Poles were forced to submerge all other considerations to the quest for national independence which took the form of frequent, spontaneous and unsuccessful revolts. As an obstacle to Prussia's Drang nach Osten and a check on Russian ambitions in Europe, Poland earned the enmity of her neighbors. The Prussians pledged to liquidate Poland "in name and fame"(1), while the Russians characterized the Poles as the "Judas of Slavdom,"(2) a French "watchdog"(3) on the East, or as a "snake spouting its venom at us."(4)

Poland was unable to restore its political identity until the simultaneous defeat of both Germany and Russia in the First World War. With it revived in a secularized version Poland's view of itself as a "key to Europe," indispensable for the balance of power on the entire continent.(5) While in Western Europe, the supposed beneficiaries of Poland's mission regarded Poland as a useful ornament to any anti-German coalition, but never as a cornerstone of European security. The Polish state was to function as a buffer between Germany and Russia, a kind

1

of early warning device for either a German or Russian breakout. The British, for example, favored Poland's independence since the Congress of Vienna in 1815, but considered that Poland should be a second-rate power incapable of pursuing its own ambitions. "There are few virtues the Poles do not possess," British Prime Minister Churchill once remarked, adding "there are few mistakes they ever avoided."(6) Britain was consistently "pro-Polish" and just as consistently "refused [Poland] all which was necessary for its existence."(7)

In modern times, the international system for Europe most favored by the Poles was that created by the Treaty of Versailles. It had the advantages of appealing to the Poles' national pride and of satisfying their political aspirations. Under it, Poland in close alliance with France played an instrumental role in containing Germany and holding Russia away from the European political scene. Such a security system depended on the military strength of France and Poland and could function only at the expense of Poland's big neighbors.

It is not surprising, therefore, that Soviet Russia was determined from the outset to change the international order in Europe that held her in a position similar to that of Russia before Peter the Great pierced his "window to Europe" to end Moscow's isolation. By invading Poland in 1920, Lenin hoped to destroy the Peace of Versailles. This first attempt failed, but at the end of the following decade the Soviets succeeded, this time in conjunction with Nazi Germany. For both Germany and Russia, Versailles Europe symbolized defeat, humiliation and insecurity. Thus, regardless of their mutual animosity, Nazi Germany and Stalinist Russia combined to overturn the effects of World War I, including the reconstituted Polish state.

In August, 1939, they concluded the Molotov-Ribbentrop Pact to partition Poland for the fourth time in history. Six weeks later, when the dismemberment was practically complete, Soviet Foreign Minister Molotov declared that with "one swift blow to Poland, first by the German Army and then by the Red Army . . . nothing was left of this ugly offspring of the Versailles Treaty."(8) In the Reichstag, Hitler made a similar statement: "Poland of the Versailles Treaty will never rise again. This is guaranteed by two of the largest states in the world."(9)

Quite naturally, the Poles had looked to France and Britain for protection. Clearly, Warsaw had learned nothing from the Czechoslovak experience at the hands of the West European powers at Munich the year before. "Neither British nor French guarantees were of help to Poland," Molotov observed, "To this day, in fact, nobody knows what these 'guarantees' were."(10)

In defeat, the Polish leadership fled to France and then to Britain, forming a government-in-exile whose guiding concept became that of the "two enemies."(11) It was based on the expectation that Germany and Russia both would be defeated, as they were in the First World War, and that the Western powers would be willing to help restore Poland as it was during the time of the Polish-Lithuanian coalition.

The Soviet attack on Finland in November, 1939, was seen by the Polish government-in-exile as a splendid opportunity to apply the two-enemies concept. The top priority became the involvement of Great Britain in war with Soviet Russia. For that reason the London Poles were eager to send the Polish troops under their command to assist Finland against Russia, expecting Great Britain to follow. Britain had no objections in principle to the continuation of the Polish-Russian war on Finland's behalf, but Finland's capitulation in March, 1940, and the Nazi triumph in Norway a month later, a campaign to which a Polish division was committed against the Germans, prevented it; the Anglo-Soviet military confrontation never materialized.

The government-in-exile never was able to correct its unrealistic view of the international balance of forces during World War II, an infirmity that ultimately facilitated the Soviet task of gaining the diplomatic isolation of the London Poles. With the Nazi attack on Russia in June, 1941, the Soviet Union became a full-fledged member in the anti-Nazi coalition. Poland's position as the privileged allied partner on Germany's east was fatally undercut.

The two-enemies policy was the primary obstacle to Polish-Soviet reconciliation during the visit of General Wladislaw Sikorski, prime minister of the exiled government, to Moscow in December. Stalin at the time professed a desire to see Poland "big and strong, stronger than ever before" as a protection for Russia against Germany. As Sikorski noted, the Soviet Union favored permanent reduction of the "power of Germany whatever its form of government and he (Stalin) added that he put no trust even in so-called 'German Communists'."(12) As for Sikorski, he put his entire trust in Great Britain and the United States, expecting that Russia would emerge from the struggle weak and paralyzed and that Poland would replace Russia as the principal power in Eastern Europe. His visit to the Soviet Union before the surge of the Nazi attack had been arrested provided Sikorski an extraordinary opportunity for a flexible diplomacy corresponding to Poland's geopolitical position "between East and West." He could have freed the Polish issue from British politics and gained leverage both in London and in Moscow. He did not.

The London Poles hoped that the postwar international system would be a replica of Versailles Europe where Poland would play a significantly enlarged role. They failed to see that Britain, their patron, preferred an alternative arrangement, similar to the one produced by the Congress of Vienna, whereby Eastern Europe would play a diminished international role and be placed under the supervision of several larger states. On August 1, 1941, The Times declared that the "Treaty of Vienna of 1815 was realistic and free of abstract principles so characteristic of the Versailles Treaty... Some leadership in Eastern Europe in the future must replace the chaos of the last twenty years."

Sikorski did accept, however, Churchill's notion that it was not necessary to obtain from Moscow any firm commitments on a postwar arrangement--believing, that Russia's enfeebled condition after the war would render superfluous any such agreements made during it. As had his predecessors from the time of the Napoleonic wars, Sikorski turned exclusively to the West for guarantees of Polish security, adding to the long list of misfortunes which have befallen Poland since the end of the Eighteenth Century. And like most Polish politicians at the time, he could not foresee that Poland's real choice was not between Great Britain and Russia, but as one Soviet official noted cynically, between "Russia and Luxembourg,"(13) or between Russia and nothing at all.

Sikorski's trip to Moscow was wasted. It served to convince the Russians that the best way for them to attain their security objectives in Europe was through a fundamental reordering of the Polish state, regardless of the cost.

The impression of common purpose created by the Moscow meeting did not endure. There were disagreements concerning the Polish Army that was to be formed in the Soviet Union from able-bodied Poles caught up on the Soviet side of the line after the 1939 partition. The Russians continued to dismiss the Sikorski government's claim to Poland's pre-1939 frontiers. Finally, the Soviets were exposed as having murdered thousands of Polish officers in the forest at Katyn, a revelation that precipitated the suspension of relations between Moscow and the Polish government in London, relations that had been restored in July, 1941. From the Soviet point of view, the "two enemies" theory implied a convergence of Polish and Nazi war aims, providing Moscow with a pretext to label the London Poles "Hitler's collaborators."(14)

As a way of increasing the international leverage of Eastern Europe, the Poles in London advocated the idea of regional federation. The Poles naturally looked southward to Czechoslovakia, especially since the Czechoslovak government in exile gave indications of some interest in the idea. As Czechoslovak President Eduard Benes explained:

> . . . neither Poland nor Czechoslovakia will be able
> to continue living separately from one another as was
> the case after the war of 1914. Even after the defeat
> of Germany, Europe will still be divided between big
> political and economic blocs. The Poles and the
> Czechoslovaks will come out of this war rather weak-
> ened, and situated as they are between Germany and
> Russia, it will be their imperative task, imposed by
> reasons both political nd economic, at least to try to
> create in Central Europe a bloc composed at first of
> their two countries and sufficiently strong to give
> their two peoples a minimum of security. (15)

In June, 1942, after about a year of negotiations, "both governments (in exile) reached agreement with regard to a number of principles of the projected Confederation." These included the establishment of a "common policy with regard to foreign affairs, defense, economic and financial matters, social questions, transportation, posts and telegraphs." A "common general staff" was to "assure the means of defense" and the coordination of a "policy of foreign trade and custom tariffs" as well as a number of other technical matters. The confederation was to be a loose union between the two sovereign states--Czechoslovakia and Poland--instead of the tripartite Czecho-Slovak-Polish federation the Poles preferred.

The reluctance of the Czechoslovaks to agree to a closer union with Poland had several causes. First, even in a two-part federation, Poland would be dominant; that, in fact, was Sikorski's intention. The second cause was related to a difference in attitude between Poland and Czechoslovakia toward both Soviet Russia and the Western powers. While Czechoslovakia felt it had been sold out at Munich by France and Great Britain, it had no pressing reasons to be apprehensive about Russia. Poland, on the other hand, had been stabbed in the back by the Russians, while the Western powers were at least pretending to act on her behalf. Thus, the representatives of neither country could agree on the extent to which Russia was a friend or an enemy, or on how much they should rely on the West. Contributing to the misunderstandings between the two governments was a dispute over a Silesian border area seized by Poland in the immediate aftermath of the Munich Pact that sanctioned the dismemberment of Czechoslovakia.

Soviet reaction to the proposed confederation was decidedly negative. Russia was opposed to "all such pacts which aimed at shaping the future, and in particular . . . agreements to which she was not a party," the Soviet ambassador explained to the Polish government in London. The Soviets were objecting to the very basis on which the confederation had been proposed. Its success would have meant increased resistance to Soviet penetration into these countries, and from Moscow's point of view it resembled no more than another version of the cordon sanitaire.

Moscow exerted pressure on the Czechs to persuade them that it was in their best interests to stay as free as possible from purely Polish concerns. Bargaining continued up to April, 1943, when the Soviet Union suspended relations with the Polish government in London. The Czechoslovak government immediately terminated all negotiations concerning the proposed confederation.(16) Thus, Sikorski's designs were checked by Stalin and once again the Poles were on their own vis-a-vis Soviet Russia.

## Alliance with the East

The concept of Poland's foreign policy elaborated by the pro-Soviet Poles differed from the London perspective in two essential points.

First of all, the Polish Communists and their followers assumed that the future Polish state must be firmly pro-Soviet if only as a means of protecting against absorption of Poland into the U.S.S.R. as a constituent Soviet republic, a course of action advocated by Lenin in 1920. Were Stalin to be without any reliable group of Poles willing to defend Soviet security interests against Germany, or the establishment of a rump state reminiscent of the dwarfish Kingdom of Poland that followed the Congress of Vienna. In their opinion, the war with Nazi Germany had resulted in a convergence of Polish and Russian interests, an outstanding opportunity to resolve common problems and establish permanent ties of friendship and mutual concerns with Russia.

Instead of trying to limit the Soviet role in post-war Europe, the Polish Left envisioned a substantial increase in such involvement. Thus Poland's international leverage would be magnified through an alliance with the strongest continental state. It also would be an occasion to reduce the power of Germany-considered by both Russia and Poland as a mortal enemy of all Slavic people. Post-war Poland, then, was to become the Soviet "watchdog" in the West, yet the "Soviet Poles" expected to exercise a considerable degree of freedom to act as a sovereign nation enjoying friendly relations with the United States, Great Britain and France.(17)

Secondly, the reorientation of Poland's foreign policy from pro-Western to pro-Soviet could be achieved only through a re-examination of the territorial, political, and ethnic framework of the Polish state.

Since either the Versailles alternative was too ambitious for Moscow, and the Kingdom of Poland version would be insufficient to sustain independence, the Polish Left resurrected another model: Piast Poland, which would have the essential territorial characteristics of the Polish state from the time of its inception in the second half of the Tenth Century until the emergence of the Polish-Lithuanian alliance at the end of the Fourteenth Century.

As for the ethnic composition of the new Piast Poland, the notion of an exclusively Polish state was fully adopted as a solution to Poland's persistent domestic weakness as well as conflict with Russia over the control of Ukrainians, Byelorussians and Lithuanians.

When combined with the concept of Piast Poland, the principle of an ethnic state--long the program of the National Democratic Party (Endeks)--meant that the Poles would have to relinquish their claims to territories east of the Curzon Line and reclaim western territories long ago lost to the Germans. This would mean roughly a Poland with the Oder-Neisse as its western boundary and the Curzon Line as its eastern border.

Further, according to this view, Poland's principle international role would no longer be that of a shield for Western
civilization, but, in cooperation with other Slavic countries, a
check on a resurgence of German nationalism. Close collaboration with Russia was seen as the cornerstone of Poland's
foreign policy, but not at the expense of independence. At the
same time, the Left realized that the success of its scheme
depended on a post-war system of security and cooperation
embracing all of Europe. In the case of a division of Europe
into antagonistic blocs, Moscow would reduce Poland's independence to a minimum and the Western powers eventually would
bestow on Germany the key role in an anti-Soviet coalition.(18)
The division of Europe would create a need for a strong Germany
(Eastern Europe being in Soviet hands) as a barrier against
Russia and would "result in establishing Germany as a political
and military power to serve as the outpost of anti-Soviet
policy."(19) The Polish Left, fully comprehended the implications for Poland of a Europe of blocs: Poland would lose its
international importance and the Polish issue would be subordinated to the solution of the German problem.

In any event, it was well understood by the Polish Socialists and nationalistic Communists that there was no alternative
to a pro-Soviet stance. Not only had the Red Army liberated
Poland from Nazi occupation, but it was plain that Poland had no
chance of securing strong support from the United States and
Britain. In addition, there was a realization that the West's
wartime diplomacy toward Soviet Russia had been characterized by
an oversimplified dichotomy which practically excluded bargaining: either yielding to Russian demands or entering into
war over them. Thus, even as a Soviet satellite, but formally
sovereign and in size co-equal to other European states, Poland
emerged from the war in much better shape than ever was advocated by the British government which supported Soviet territorial claims against Poland but was reluctant to compensate the
Poles with German territory east of the Oder-Neisse Line.

In its over-all appraisal, the Left developed the internationally feasible alternative of a Poland secured by the Russian
need to have a buffer zone, against Germany in particular and
the West in general. Simultaneously, the Left succeeded in
convincing the Russians that the forceful incorporation of
Poland into the Soviet Union would be self-defeating. For these
reasons, the Left must be distinguished from the London Poles
who were poor politicians whose military forecasts were wrong,
whose diplomatic calculations were unrealistic and whose attitudes were inflexible.

Above all, the London Poles had a wildly exaggerated
impression of Poland's international importance and its impact
on global stability. Their errors stemmed in large measure from
an ultra-nationalistic reading of Polish history (a legacy of
the partitions when the study of history was a tool for preserving national culture and pride). This lack of proportion was
reflected forcefully in the comments of Stanislaw Mikolajczyk,
the premier of the exiled government in London, who warned

Western leaders that the Polish problem contained "the germs of worldwide conflict." He added:

> It should be clear that if Poland were not to regain
> her independence or if brutal and ruthless conditions
> were imposed upon her against the will of the Polish
> people, Europe would have to face the prospect of a
> new and dangerous conflict. I am not one of those who
> continually harp on historical comparisons and who
> draw too far-reaching conclusions from the past, but I
> think I should remind my readers of the fact that
> when, after the Napoleonic Wars, Poland was wronged by
> the Treaty of Vienna of 1815, she refused to be
> content with this solution and opposed it for 100
> years until her claims were made good by the Treaty of
> Versailles. (20)

He no doubt had forgotten that the frequent Polish uprisings during the Nineteenth Century failed to induce any Western state to provide meaningful support for Poland and that no major war in Europe ever was fought for the Polish cause. No gun was fired by the Western powers on behalf of Poland in September, 1939.

Still, the London Poles continued to believe Poland was a major power. General Anders, commander of the Second Polish Corps fighting alongside American and British troops in Western Europe, informed Churchill that after the defeat of Germany, the Poles would beat the Russians.(21) He must have expected a miracle.

It should have been clear that foreigners would determine Poland's government, territorial configuration and socio-economic system. "Never in the history of human conflict was the fate of so many decided so bluntly and by so few."(22) Such was the conclusion of the Second World War for the nation whose contribution to victory over Germany was exceeded only by that of the United States, Russia and Great Britain.

## Security via Stalinization

While the eastern border of Poland was established through bilateral Polish-Soviet negotiations, the Soviets deliberately left open the question of Poland's western border. The inconclusive status of the Oder-Neisse Line provided the Soviets with diplomatic flexibility when dealing with the Western powers over the German issue and with political leverage on both the Poles and East German Communists, the agents of Soviet interest in Germany.

With regard to Poland, the Potsdam Conference provided that the final decision on the western border had to await the peace conference formally concluding the war and that the Polish provisional government, whose members were selected by the Russians with a few officials co-opted from the ranks of the London Poles, must "as soon as possible" organize "free and unfettered elections."

The Poles soon discovered that these two provisions were mutually exclusive and that a choice had to be made between the security of the Polish state and the domestic system preferred by most Poles. Warsaw realized that the result of elections would determine not only the attitude of the Soviet Union and the United States toward Poland and consequently toward the Oder-Neisse Line. From the Polish point of view, the main issue was whether the Soviet Union or the Western powers were more likely to champion Poland's territorial claims against Germany, as if the Poles had any real choice at all.

Knowing that "free and unfettered elections" would turn Poland to the West, Stalin instructed Poland's President Boleslaw Bierut that the "elections must be won before the elections."(23) Motivated by their own interests and the fear of Soviet intervention, the Communists in Warsaw had no alternative but to violate the election provisions of the Potsdam Agreement. Still, it was an open question as to how serious a violation it was going to be. The Warsaw government had to provide Moscow with convincing evidence that it was capable of protecting Soviet security interests, knowing that the price of falsifying the elections would be international isolation, rejection by the Polish nation and an uncertain future owing to the capricious nature of Soviet tutelage.

Perhaps no one was really serious about post-war elections in Poland. At the time the "free and unfetterred elections" provision was written, Poland was occupied by Russian troops and it would have been naive to expect the Soviets to restrict their influence in Poland in response to the wishes of the Polish people. The Western leaders were well acquainted with the kind of elections conducted in the Soviet Union since the Bolshevik takeover. One iron rule of such elections is that they produce no political change. For the United States and Great Britain the election provision was no more than a face-saving device; it provided them with a defense against the accusation that they had given Poland away to Stalinist Russia.

The arrangement was equally convenient for the Soviet government. "Winning" the Polish elections was a relatively easy task, considering the massive presence of the Red Army and the effectiveness of the Polish secret police under the control of the NKVD. The Potsdam Agreement failed to provide for any international supervision of elections in Poland.

A closely related issue involved the fate of the 250,000-man Polish Army in the West, which had no intention of disbanding. Its return intact to Poland would threaten the security of Soviet occupation forces and could also provoke a civil war. The decision of the "London government" to preserve an independent Polish government and its refusal to repatriate the Polish Army because such a repatriation would be "cloaked with uncertain consequences"(24) must have been welcomed by the newly installed Warsaw authorities.

In any case, Warsaw's invitation to the Polish Armed Forces to return home coincided with a propaganda campaign accusing them of supporting terrorism in Poland, while Molotov proclaimed the Polish troops were a potential disturbance to the peace.(25)

Only 17 percent of the Polish soldiers did return home, mainly because Britain was not interested in securing international guarantees for their safety in a country already known for political murders committed by the secret police.(26)

Thus, allegedly by its own volition, did Poland become a pro-Soviet and Communist-dominated state, once again left with neither the support nor the understanding of the West. The Western powers began to regard Poland through the prism of their relations with Soviet Russia, making no effort to distinguish between Soviet objectives and the choices available to the Poles.

Necessity dictated a clearer definition of relations with Poland's new international sponsor. Nominally, Poland was a fully independent sovereign country, which, however, could not afford the privilege of free elections.(27) It was evident that Moscow was intent on introducing the Soviet domestic model into Poland, but the actual degree of Poland's international independence was neither defined nor was there any precedent in this respect.

It is not surprising, therefore, that the first demand the Warsaw government addressed to Moscow was that both countries formally regulate their relations according to the principles of international law, including mutual respect for sovereignty, territorial integrity and equality.

Wladislaw Gomulka, vice premier and first secretary of the Polish Workers Party, publicly invited the Soviet Union to conclude with Poland a treaty of friendship similar to the ones Moscow signed with Czechoslovakia in 1943 and with France in 1944.(28) It was implied that the relations existing between the Soviet authorities and the Union of Polish Patriots as well as the Polish Committee of National Liberation were not to be a substitute for a bilateral agreement regulated by international law. The Polish authorities also were seeking this way some degree of protection against the arbitrary conduct of Moscow. Like the rest of the Polish nation, the Communists, too, were victimized by Soviet paranoia, particularly in the 1930s when

Stalin's purges decimated the ranks of the Polish Communist
Party.
    As a matter of fact, the only members of the pre-war
Communist Party who survived the Great Purge of the 1930s were
those who were serving time in Polish prisons and thus were
beyond the reach of the NKVD's henchmen.  There were few politicians better prepared by experience for dealing with Moscow.
    The first decisive step toward international legal recog-
nition of Poland took place on January 4, 1945, with an exchange
of ambassadors between Poland and the Soviet Union.  Before the
Polish mission was allowed to arrive in Moscow, however, the
Soviets waited for the end of the Potsdam Conference and a
clarification of the Western powers' attitudes.  Later, after
brief negotiations the first post-war Polish-Soviet treaty was
concluded August 16, 1945.(29)  Except for a detailed description of the new Polish-Soviet border, its provisions differed
little from the ones decided upon in Moscow in July of the
preceding year.  No mention whatsoever was made of Soviet
support for Poland's new western borders.
    A provision of key importance declared that the treaty was
an implementation of the Yalta decisions on Poland.(30)  So now
it was not the Soviet Union alone, but all of the Big Three who
were the chief guarantors of Polish independence.  In this way a
clear distinction was drawn between the authority of Polish
wartime organizers in Russia and the legitimacy of the post-war
Polish government.
    But nothing could change the painful reality that the
domestic affairs of Poland were closely controlled by the
Soviets and that Poland's sovereignty over the Oder-Neisse
territories was deliberately limited by the Soviet's interest in
the economic wealth of this area.  Stalin suggested joint
Polish-Soviet ownership of the Silesian coal mines, but facing
the united opposition of the Polish delegation, dropped his plan
and instructed Molotov to prepare a new proposal that would take
Poland's sovereignty into account.  Molotov estimated the total
economic value of Poland's former eastern territories at $3.5
billion, while assessing at $9.5 billion the value of Poland's
newly acquired western territories.  He admitted that the
Soviets had managed to remove industrial equipment worth $500
million before the Polish administration took over, but determined that the Poles were still getting a bargain.  In addition,
he argued, the Soviet Union had agreed at Potsdam that reparations for Poland were to be taken from the Soviet share, thus,
the Soviets deserved some extra benefit from Silesia.
    In the final agreement, the Soviet Union renounced any
right to claim German property in Poland and promised to furnish
Poland 50,000 German prisoners of war who were to help in the
extraction of coal for Russia.  Poland agreed to deliver coal at
the price of $1.25 a ton--"without a profit and without a loss,"
according to Beirut.(31)  There was evidently no political
limitation imposed on Polish sovereignty over the recorded
western territories only a heavy economic price attached to
Soviet guardianship of the second "Piast Poland."

The new authorities were inclined to meet even excessive
Soviet demands in the hope of preserving Poland's nominal
independence. They reassured themselves that when viewed in a
larger historical perspective the price paid for Polish statehood would be seen as one the nation could afford. Similarly
they justified their own ascent to power as a patriotic act
consistent with the best long-term interests of Poland.

Before long it was apparent that a Europe of blocs was
indeed forming. In a speech at Fulton, Missouri, on March 5,
1946, Churchill, by then a private citizen, spoke of aggression
in Europe. In the presence of President Truman, Churchill
called on "English-speaking" peoples to stem the "expansive and
proselytizing tendencies" of Russia. Europe, Churchill said,
had been divided into two parts: ". . . from Stettin in the
Baltic to Trieste in the Adriatic, an iron curtain has descended
across the continent." Putting Poland on the side of the
aggressors, Churchill said "The Russian-dominated Polish government has been encouraged to make enormous and wrongful inroads
upon Germany, and mass expulsions of millions of Germans on a
scale grievous and undreamed-of are now taking place."(32)

Churchill's "Iron Curtain" speech had been preceded by
statements by Molotov and Stalin reinterpreting the causes of
the war. At the root of the conflict was not the traditional
German-Slavic struggle, but a class conflict between the forces
of "capitalism" and "socialism." The continued existence of an
"imperialist" camp, now under American leadership, made peaceful
coexistence impossible. The Soviet Union must be prepared for
all sorts of "surprises," Stalin concluded.(33)

At the time of Churchill's attack on the Polish government,
British hopes of influencing events in Poland had disappeared
with the exclusion of pro-British politicians from any comman-
ding role in the new Polish political set-up. For Churchill,
then, the behavior of the Warsaw regime was merely a manifestation of Russian imperialism. Churchill felt therefore that the
Western powers were under no further obligation to promote
recognition of the new Polish-German frontier. Simply put, from
the Western point of view the Oder-Neisse boundary was for a
democratic, pro-Western Poland alone.(34)

This helped the Warsaw government portray Soviet Russia as
genuinely dedicated to the advancement of Poland's cause; any
anti-Soviet sentiments on the part of the Poles were said to
have been artificially created by the opposition.(35)

In foreign affairs, the Polish government immediately
turned to Stalin, asking for a renewed pledge of support. How
he must have watched with satisfaction as his plans came to
fruition. Having been compelled by Stalin to violate the
Potsdam Agreement, the Poles had no alternative now but to seek
his protection. Still, the Poles knew that in the event of a
major East-West German trade-off, Poland and the Oder-Neisse
territories in particular, would become the chief commodity.

Not surprisingly, there was a fear that the "spirit . . .
of Munich (was) . . . striking directly at our nation."(36) Nor
could the Polish Communists have forgotten that the Russians
always valued a deal with the Germans more highly than one with

the Poles.  Such was the precedent set by Tsar Alexander I who
in 1805 concluded a secret agreement with Polish aristocrats in
Pulawy, only to change his mind as soon as an understanding with
the Prussians became possible.  The same attitude was adopted by
his Bolshevik successors, as the Molotov-Ribbentrop pact was to
prove.  Sometime later, Nikita Khrushchev related that during
his talks with Polish Communists on a visit to Poland in 1945 he
had discovered that "the treaty of 1939 had deeply wounded the
Poles and the wound was still fresh."

At the beginning of 1946, a Polish diplomat could remark
that his country's "friendship" with the Soviet Union was to be
a "fundamental principle of Polish foreign policy" but that did
not preclude Poland from having an "independent opinion" on a
number of important international issues.  "We do not want to be
an element in the game of the great powers."  Deputy Foreign
Minister Modzelewski told Secretary Bevin.(37)  Soon any idea of
balancing Soviet influence in Poland became too dangerous to
think about.  Poland was left with no alternative but incorporation into the international structure dominated by the
Soviets and the hope that Moscow's international successes would
also benefit Warsaw.

The regime increased its use of terrorist tactics against
the anti-Communist opposition in Poland, drawing from the United
States protests against the "suppression, coercion and intimi-
dation applied to the political opposition."  The Americans
pointed out, in vain, that these methods violated not only the
spirit but the letter of the Yalta and Potsdam agreements.

The chief concern of the Polish government, however, was
not placating Washington but satisfying Moscow.  In this sense
the greatest gift Warsaw could offer Stalin would be a sound
"victory" in the national elections of January, 1947.  Duti-
fully, the government coalition announced that it had won an 87-
percent majority.  The Soviet Union certified that the elections
had been democratic.  Thus was met the provision agreed upon at
Yalta and Potsdam for elections that were "free and unfettered."
In reality these terms were scarcely accurate as a description
of the elections.(38)  No sooner were the results in that the
Soviet Union announced that it considered the Oder-Neisse Line
as the "permanent" Polish-German frontier.(39)

So with the beginning of 1947 it was clear that the Warsaw
government had failed to secure for itself support and respect
in the West or situate itself politically between the superpowers.  As a natural consequence of the fraudulent elections
Communist Poland faced international isolation.  Yet neither
Washington nor London withdrew its diplomatic recognition of the
Polish regime for fear of far-reaching consequences leading
perhaps to Poland's incorporation into the U.S.S.R.

From both the political and legal points of view the Oder-
Neisse Line was still unresolved.  While the Communists could
assert that the "London" government's loyalty to the Western
allies had brought no rewards to Poland, they lacked convincing
proof that their own fealty to Soviet Russia would be properly
appreciated.  They had "won" the Polish elections, which
strengthened their grip on the country.  But they had not yet

achieved a monopoly. Accordingly, they were instructed to "clean house," that is, eliminate any form of opposition, including and especially allies like the Socialists.

Clearly, Stalin wanted additional payment for Soviet support of Poland's security. The continued "democratization"-- as the destruction of the Polish Communists' rivals was called-- merely increased the dependence of the Polish regime on Moscow.

Another factor drawing Poland toward the Soviets was what Warsaw viewed as the American policy of rebuilding of Germany's economic potential before attending to Germany's victims. The Poles argued that the economies of the East European countries deserved priority. (Yet, when U.S. Marshall Plan aid was offered to Eastern Europe, the Soviets prevailed on the Poles to reject it.) There was also a strong Polish feeling that the economic weakness would be an effective check on German nationalism. The Polish premier, Jozef Cyrankiewicz, feared that German recovery "would result in (German) hegemony in industry and the creation of a new firebrand of war."(40) An economically vital Germany has always been viewed by the Poles as a threat to their security.

Initial French reluctance to go along with the United States and Britain in aiding German reconstruction revived hopes in Warsaw for a limited partnership with a major West European state. The Polish Communists wished for a friendly reception in Paris.

There were several reasons for them to expect French interest in political collaboration. Historically, each looked toward the other in matters of security, agreeing that Germany should be weak and divided. This fundamental fear of Germany caused a division between French and Anglo-American objectives in post-war Europe. Within the Western alliance, France was weak and felt alienated; any partnership would be welcomed to increase France's international weight. There was also the fact of French distrust of its Anglo-Saxon allies who were perceived to have mistreated France and ignored French interests during the war. Disliking dependence on the United States, the French were seeking alternatives which would allow them to preserve their place in Europe. At this point, French and Polish interests converged. Finally, the exceptionally strong influence of Communists and Socialists in France could make feasible a French foreign policy based on cooperation with a Communist state.

The Poles decided to try, doubtless with Soviet approval. The Paris Peace Conference in February, 1947, was an opportunity for the Polish foreign minister to meet members of the French Cabinet and introduce a Polish proposal. Bilateral economic agreements already were in effect--both sides were satisfied with the state of their trade. A cultural program was promptly arranged. But political matters were not so simple.

Poland's offer had the appearance of innocence. Recalling the post-Versailles period, Poland proposed to continue the Franco-Polish alliance begun in 1921, but on condition that it be adapted to the new political circumstances. The purpose of the proposed revision was to strip the old treaty of its anti-Soviet features and aim it exclusively at Germany. Poland declared its willingness to support the French claim on the Saar and asked for help on the Oder-Neisse issue.(41)

If accepted, such a proposal would have made France appear as a pro-Soviet state. Warsaw pretended there was no such thing as a "Russian menace" in Europe, focusing instead on an attempt to engage France in an alliance against the just-defeated and prostrate enemy. Traditionally, the Polish-French alliance was double-edged: anti-Russian and anti-German, with neither country allied to an outside power. The proposed treaty would have had quite a different character. It would have had the effect of France's turning its back on the United States. Even that may have been acceptable, but Poland would not and could not contribute its share: that is, check Soviet influence in Eastern Europe. No matter how much the French might disagree with American policy toward Germany, it made no sense for France to attach itself to the Soviet wagon. France wanted increased independence, not an exchange of one unequal alliance for another, especially one more dangerous and unpredictable.

In making such a proposal, the Poles were acting more as Soviet agents than as custodians of Poland's interests, thereby reducing for the French the value of the offer. Another reason for the inability of France and Poland to conclude a treaty stemmed from changes in the French political situation at home. Finally, the United States, which all along had more to offer France than the Soviet Union did, initiated a policy designed to produce a Franco-German reconciliation. For Poland, that meant the end of any hope for a "Westpolitik."(42)

Consequently, the Polish Communists had to limit their political ambitions to the Soviet-controlled part of Europe. Under the banner of Slavic unity, Poland signed treaties with other East European countries, enlisting them one after the other as Poland's allies against Germany.

The treaty with the Soviet Union of April 21, 1945, pro- vided the example. The Polish-Yugoslav treaty of March 14, 1946 (terminated in 1948) was concluded for the purpose of "tight- ening the bonds of secular friendship between the brother Slav nations." It imposed the mutual obligation to "afford . . . immediate military and other assistance and support by all means" in the case of "hostilities against Germany."(43) Next came Czechoslovakia; both states found it "desirous (to) en- sur(e) the peaceful development of both Slav countries" and to protect each other against Germany as well as "any other states associated with Germany."(44) With Bulgaria, "a lasting rapprochement between these two Slavic countries" was achieved, with the proviso that "should either of the High Contracting Parties be subjected to aggression by Germany or any other state which might be associated with Germany directly or indirectly or in any other way, the other High Contracting Party shall imme- diately afford it military and other assistance and support with all the means at its disposal."(45) Exactly the same wording went into the treaties with Hungary and Romania, except, of course, for the bond of Slavic unity.(46) With these and the treaty with Russia, Poland developed a network of bilateral security arrangements which nevertheless gave no specific endorsement to Poland's claim to the Oder-Neisse territories.

Simultaneously, Moscow proceeded apace with its incorporation of Poland into the Soviet system. This process culminated in 1949, when Stalin dispatched Soviet Marshal Constantin Rokossowski to Warsaw to be commander-in-chief of the Polish armed forces. Rokossowski had been born in Warsaw, but his entire adult life, beginning with military service in the tsar's army, had been spent in Russia. He was to become a Soviet war hero in the struggle against the Germans. The fact that Rokossowski had had one Polish parent was sufficient pretext for Moscow to grant what was officially described as the Polish government's request for his "return." The Soviet Union "magnanimously" agreed and "released (Rokossowski) from service in the Red Army." He was made Minister of Defense with the rank of marshal in the Polish Army and was elevated to the Politburo of the Polish Communist Party. In fact, he became the "Soviet proconsul in Poland," in charge of destroying the last vestiges of opposition.(47)

As far as the purpose of Rokossowski's mission was concerned, Khrushchev was to explain:

> . . . it goes without saying that the reactionary forces which had come to the surface correctly understood that Rokossowski would never raise his hand against the Soviet Union, nor would he lead the Polish Army against the Soviet Army. In short, he may have been a Polish marshal, but he was also a Soviet marshal--and no one had better forget it. (48)

The most persuasive interpretation of Stalin's move to deprive Polish Communists of control of their own armed forces seems to be that Moscow had finally decided to consolidate its military borders on the Oder-Neisse Line.(49)

In these conditions, the Soviet appointment of Marshal Rokossowski to Polish office diminished the Poles' uncertainty over their western frontier. But it also meant that their national security ceased to be their own business. There was, however, a source of satisfaction: Faced with a choice between Poland and East Germany, Moscow showed a preference for Poland. This meant Moscow must have abandoned hope for a solution to the German problem that would enhance Soviets' chances for influencing developments beyond their zone of occupation. It explains why the East German Communists were compelled to accept Oder-Neisse as a permanent arrangement. During the Big Four foreign ministers' session in Paris, in May, 1949, the Soviet Union declared again that the issue of the Polish-German border had been settled conclusively at Potsdam.(50)

The "friendship" with the Soviet Union left no room for much that was Polish in post-war Poland. Polish Communists were not allowed to chart their own course to socialism. At the same time, this "friendship" was understood to mean that Polish independence would be limited for the purpose of providing Russia security vis-a-vis the West. It was not long before even the

most pro-Soviet individuals were disappointed as the notion of
an independent identity for Poland became less realistic.

This was the period of the final division of Europe. The
Paris Agreement put a cap on it, granting full independence to
the Federal Republic of Germany and allowing it to militarize.
West Germany then became a member of NATO. Such a move could
not remain unanswered. So, in addition to its bilateral
treaties, the Soviet Union organized its bloc into a single
military organization. The preamble to the Treaty of Warsaw of
May 14, 1955, stated the reason:

> The situation created in Europe by the ratification
> of the Paris agreements, which envisage the formation
> of a new military alignment in the shape of a 'Western
> European Union,' with the participation of a remilita-
> rized West Germany and the integration of the latter
> in the North Atlantic bloc . . . increases the danger
> of another war and constitutes a threat to the na-
> tional security of peaceful states. (51)

Thus, at the end of the Stalinist period, Poland found
itself completely integrated in the Soviet alliance, bereft of
the political authority or the capacity to represent Polish
national interests in international affairs.

## In Search of Collective Security

During and immediately after the Second World War two Polish governments--one entirely dependent upon the West, the other based exclusively on Soviet support--had common experiences. Each became subordinated to such an extent that its integrity was lost in the sacrifice of Polish interests to the interests of its sponsor. The result was an alienation from the Polish nation. If there was a lesson, it was to avoid entrusting Poland's international affairs exclusively to one great power.

The Cold War and Stalinism had prevented Poland from developing balanced relations with both Soviet Russia and the Western powers. Instead, Poland was bound into the Soviet web by the means of a bilateral treaty, membership in the regional security system organized and dominated by the Soviets, the transplantation of Soviet ideological, political and economic norms, imposition of a Polish government composed largely of non-Poles whose loyalties were to Moscow and divestiture from the Polish authorities of control of the country's armed forces. The differences between Poland's status and that of a Soviet republic were reduced to a minimum.

In such conditions, the October, 1956, revolt in Poland was, in effect, a reassertion of Polish independence. Still greatly reliant on its eastern neighbor, the country nevertheless emerged from the revolt more nearly capable of pursuing its own goals. High among them was seen to be the elaboration of a Europe-wide security system as a substitute for bloc politics. In this way, it was expected, Poland's subordination to Moscow would be lessened and strict international constraints would be imposed on both German states.

Poland's main preoccupation was Germany. Under the Potsdam Agreement, this traditional enemy was condemned to a permanent weakness secured by demilitarization, democratization and the break-up of its cartels. Germany was defeated and helpless, and such a state of affairs was to become permanent. Europe without Germany as a strong political, military and economic power was a pleasant prospect for the Poles.

Accordingly, restoration of Germany was a source of deep concern. Conflicting attitudes toward German reunification were to be at the root of subsequent disagreements between Warsaw and Bonn. In the view of the Federal Republic, satisfactory solution of the German question was a precondition to peace and concord in Europe and must be given priority. Poland understandably based its European policy on a contrary principle: The German problem, its solution--in light of the historical experience of European nations--must be subordinated to European security.

When Poland managed to enhance its control over foreign policy after October, 1956, it found itself faced in the West with a remilitarized Federal Republic officially committed to territorial revisions at Poland's expense. Furthermore, some West German politicians and military experts were advocating the acquisition of nuclear weapons to strengthen the Bundeswehr.

Poland took the lead among the East bloc countries in an effort to stop Germany from becoming a nuclear power.

Under the circumstances, Polish and Soviet security aims appeared broadly similar. Both regimes advocated a collective security system in Europe that would recognize the division of Germany and legitimize Communist control over Eastern Europe. Warsaw, however, pursued a more nuanced approach. While the Soviet Union promoted the idea of a general security conference in Europe, Poland appeared to favor a "narrowing" of the issue in a geographical and military sense. It proposed partial, temporary solutions.(52)

Between 1957 and 1964, Poland conducted a semi-independent foreign policy, first as the advocate of a total removal of nuclear weapons from Central Europe and later as the proponent of a freeze on nuclear arms at the heart of the continent. Both plans envisioned preservation of America's active involvement in European affairs not only to contain German nationalism but to deprive the Soviet Union of a monopoly of power in Europe. The Soviets, by contrast, held that the United States had no legitimate security concerns in Europe.

Several times during the second half of 1957 Polish Foreign Minister Adam Rapacki mentioned the desirability of creating an atom-free zone in Central Europe, but a detailed formulation of this idea was not made available until February, 1958. In a memorandum, the government of the Polish People's Republic explained:

> The proposed zone should include the territory of
> Poland, Czechoslovakia, the German Democratic Republic
> and the German Federal Republic. In this territory
> nuclear weapons would neither be manufactured nor
> stockpiled, the equipment and installations designed
> for their servicing would not be located there, the
> use of nuclear weapons against the territory of this
> zone would be prohibited. (53)

Poland was asking for the removal of nuclear weapons from three Warsaw Pact states and one member of the Atlantic Alliance. The combined territories of Poland, Czechoslovakia and East Germany covered some 550,000 square kilometers; their populations totaled some fifty-eight million people. In West Germany, a population of some fifty-five million inhabited about 250,000 square kilometers. The average depth of the proposed zone was 300 kilometers on the western side, 700 kilometers on the eastern.(54) The zone to be affected was the most sensitive in Europe since it is where the armies of the blocs had faced each other since the end of the war.

The proposal contained two interrelated elements. First of all, it was addressed to the four states of the zone. None possessed nuclear arms and each was being asked to renounce any future production, importation or control of such weapons. Second, it was addressed to the nuclear powers who would have to work out an agreement governing withdrawal of their nuclear forces. Afterwards, they were to "undertake the obligation to

respect the status of the zone as an area in which there would
be no nuclear weapons and against which nuclear weapons should
not be used."(55)

It was, therefore, a plan of partial demilitarization
which, in Warsaw's eyes, had several advantages: It offered
protection against nuclear attack to the nations of the zone and
it would be the first serious step toward the solution of
security in Europe.  In addition, Poland emphasized that the
Federal Republic should never gain access to nuclear arms.  If
the West Germans ever did, Poland warned, the Warsaw Pact
countries would take "appropriate steps to strengthen their own
security."(56)

Neither Poland, Czechoslovakia, East Germany nor the
Federal Republic of Germany was able to decide on its own
whether it was safe or desirable to remove all nuclear arms from
Central Europe.  Since the military and political implications
of partial demilitarization would have a direct bearing on the
security of the United States and Russia, the implementation of
the Rapacki Plan required the cooperation of the superpowers.

Poland's role virtually ended with the announcement of the
plan.  Poland, of course, could renounce its own nuclear
ambitions, as could the other Warsaw Pact members of the
proposed zone.  But such renunciations would ring hollow since
the Soviet Union was eager to share nuclear weapons with no one,
especially the Poles who in October, 1956, had threatened to
fight the Russians.  Unlike the United States, the Soviets could
not fully trust their allies.  This, after all, was less than
two years after the Hungarian revolution as well.

The probable outcome of the Rapacki Plan's implementation
would have been advantageous to the Soviets.  The nuclear forces
of the United States and Britain would be removed from West
Germany, while the West Germans themselves would be blocked from
nuclear armaments.  Additionally, this would deprive Russia's
satellites of the justification for demanding such weapons
themselves as a defense against German territorial claims.

Still, Poland's own interest in a Central European nuclear-
free zone should not be forgotten.  The plan included the
prospect of a partial withdrawal of Soviet troops from Polish
territory.  Already, in October, 1956, Gomulka had requested the
complete removal of Soviet units from Poland, but retreated
under Soviet pressure and fear of Germany.  Under the Rapacki
Plan, a nuclear-free West Germany could no longer be regarded as
an extraordinary threat and the Soviet military presence in
Poland would consist of conventional forces only.  Moreover,
Russia would be deprived of the right to use nuclear weapons in
Poland.  Whatever the military value of such an arrangement, it
would make the Polish-Soviet partnership more equal.  In other
words, if there were to be global gains for Moscow from the
plan, Poland could at least count on some regional advantages.

Rapacki admitted his plan had been "agreed upon . . . by
the other members of the Warsaw Pact."(57)  It could not be
otherwise.  No such initiative could be taken by a junior member
of the Warsaw Pact without gaining the advance approval of the
senior member, especially a proposal affecting European secur-

ity. Minister Rapacki did not have to wait long for the Soviets to express publicly their full support for his plan. They declared a readiness to participate in all negotiations dealing with the proposal and even before Warsaw was able to provide a detailed elaboration of the project, Moscow indicated it was willing to abide by its provisions.(58) Though Poland hoped to play the role of mediator between East and West, its initiatives could not be viewed as other than representing the interests of the Soviet bloc, and more specifically those of the Soviet Union.

As to notions of developing a European security system, Pierre Hassner asked correctly: By

> 'European security system,' do we mean a 'European system of security' or a 'system of European Security?' Is the method, the system, to be European, or only the result, the security? Are the Europeans to be security producers, or just consumers? Are we to aim at the security of the Europeans, by the Europeans, for the Europeans, or is Europe's security to be provided basically by the two great powers, with or without the representation or the participation of the Europeans? (59)

There was the rub. The Poles were promoting a solution whereby the superpowers were to act as guarantors of the security of the European states. Thus all Polish proposals concerning the solution of European problems could only be extensions of Soviet foreign policy in Europe and vis-a-vis the United States. The Rapacki Plan was rejected by the Western powers primarily because of its potential effects on the global balance of power. For the Western bloc, European--that is, regional-- and global political and strategic systems were inseparable.

The Western decision to reject the Rapacki Plan was also based on military ground. The military experts pointed out that under the plan the Soviet Union would acquire a considerable strategic advantage in Europe. It was generally conceded that Soviet conventional forces were superior to those of the NATO countries, and the function of American nuclear weapons in Western Europe was to fill this gap. The West saw its nuclear force as defensive and designed to sustain an over-all balance of power in Europe.

In proposing a partial demilitarization limited to Central Europe, the Poles argued that the implementation of their plan could have no impact upon the global balance of power. In fact, denuclearization of Central Europe would increase Soviet security and enhance this preponderance of Soviet power in the region without any corresponding gains for the West. NATO nuclear forces (whose role was to contain Soviet conventional forces) would have to be removed to the very edge of the continent, 1,000 kilometers from the Western border of the Soviet Union, while the Red Army would remain in the heart of Europe enjoying protection from nuclear attack. In the Rapacki Plan, Moscow was eager to assign twice as much depth to the Eastern side as to the Western segment since this would provide better protection against any attack from the West.

Furthermore, the NATO countries could scarcely ignore the unequal depth of the blocs, which in military terms meant that the nuclear forces of the Western alliance would have restricted room for maneuver. With more than 1,500 kilometers between Moscow and their western border, the Russians faced no such disadvantage.

The final argument of a military nature concerned compliance and verification. Any available system of verification would be deficient in peacetime, and in war there was no guarantee that nuclear arms would not be employed in Central Europe, despite the assurances by Nikolai Bulganin, the Soviet leader, provided to West German Chancellor Konrad Adenauer that there would never be any military need to use such weapons within the denuclearized zone.(60) For all practical purposes the effectiveness of the Rapacki Plan could be secured only by goodwill. In light of recent Soviet history, this was a risk the West was unwilling to take.

The most vocal political objections to the Rapacki Plan were expressed by the Federal Republic of Germany. Bonn's dislike for the proposal stemmed from its reunification--first position. For the West Germans the political and territorial status quo was discriminatory and the primary source of tension in Europe. If the Polish government wanted to improve conditions in Europe, the West Germans said, it should attempt to solve the German issue. The Rapacki Plan, however, called for the perpetuation of the status quo (the indisputable "acceptance of reality," as Warsaw used to call it), including full recognition of the East German regime, renunciation of any territorial claims including the "right to the homeland" and recognition of Polish borders.(61) This was unacceptable to Bonn, since such an arrangement could only deepen division and heighten tension in Europe.

The Polish assessment of European conditions was quite different, of course. The status quo was regarded as the best guarantee for peace. The Cold War, in turn, was sustained by West German determination to absorb the German Democratic Republic and put into question the Oder-Neisse Line. Like the West Germans, Poland recognized the relationship between the German issue and European security, but the proposed order of developments envisaged was exactly the reverse of Bonn's. For Adenauer, ". . . the right to a homeland must be recognized. The people must be allowed to go back, and also the economic integration of those territories (east of the Oder-Neisse line) must be ensured. Once these two questions are solved and consequently the indispensable easing of tensions between Poland and us has occurred . . . then the political questions will solve themselves."(62) But according to Rapacki, the "first step" should be the relaxation of tension and then would the key to the German problem be easily found.

Politically, the Rapacki Plan contained the seeds of German neutralization, and thus an important goal of Soviet post-war foreign policy. In that light, many in Western Europe, fearing

that the neutralization of Germany would encourage the United
States to withdraw from the continent, viewed the plan as
neither useful nor desirable.(63)   Central Europe was too vital
to risk experimentation.

The Rapacki Plan failed.  Still, the Soviets--and, to be
sure,--the Poles--were no less interested in preventing the
Federal Republic of Germany from becoming a nuclear power nor
were they any less eager to impede the continuing integration of
Bonn into the Western bloc.  Poland was to devise new plans.

The first called for the improvement of bilateral relations
and before long an economic agreement was concluded with the
West Germans.  To obtain it, Warsaw dropped its insistence on
any political preconditions and was willing to exchange trade
missions, granting them broad consular authority.  This was,
according to Trybuna Ludu, a "step in the direction of normalization and stabilization of peaceful relations in Europe."(64)
Warsaw expected the economic agreement to be followed by political moves.  But the Polish government had miscalculated.
Within several months, Gomulka was forced to admit that no
political progress had resulted from the establishment of trade
relations with West Germany.  So Poland turned directly to the
superpowers in a second attempt to inhibit any West German
nuclear ambitions.

This new Polish initiative, which became known as the
Gomulka Plan, proposed a freeze on nuclear weapons in Central
Europe--West Germany, the German Democratic Republic, Poland and
Czechoslovakia.  The key provision of the plan stated that the:

> Parties maintaining armed forces in the area of the
> proposed freeze of armaments would undertake obli-
> gations not to produce, not to introduce or import,
> not to transfer to other parties in the area or to
> accept from other parties in the area the aforemen-
> tioned nuclear and thermonuclear weapons. (65)

The basic aim of the Gomulka Plan was to deprive the West
Germans of nuclear arms while allowing the nuclear powers to
perpetuate their stalemate.  Unlike its predecessor, the Rapacki
Plan, no protection against nuclear attack was offered and no
demilitarization was asked.  Implementation would involve
appropriate declarations by all states concerned and the establishment of a system of international controls.  The Gomulka
Plan never received serious consideration in the West.

It was founded on the same assumption as Rapacki's--that
the regional and global aspects of the East-West balance of
power were divisible.  This time, Warsaw deliberately overlooked
not only Soviet superiority in conventional weapons, but also
the nuclear buildup in European Russia where most Soviet medium-
range ballistic missiles were deployed.  "In effect," concluded
Zbigniew Brzezinski, "the Polish proposal meant a freeze on
further American security measures in Europe (since Germany is
the principal locus of American forces), with the Soviet Union
remaining immune to such restrictions."(66)

The basic political objections also were unchanged. The Federal Republic of Germany refused to recognize East Germany, even indirectly, or to accept the territorial status quo. Moreover, Bonn added a new precondition for detente by requiring every political move to contribute to the enlargement of the sphere of "human rights," giving rise to the accusation that West Germany had adopted the former American policy of "liberalization" of Eastern Europe. With respect to the territorial issues, the Federal Republic set its policy into a formula of status quo minus; that is, opposition to any action aimed at strengthening existing national frontiers and the so-called junctim became a standard for evaluation of all security proposals in Europe. Bonn wanted every such program to advance German reunification.(67)

This was unacceptable to Poland, whose policy was firmly based on the assumption that the "recognition of the existence of the German Democratic Republic and respect of its sovereign rights was . . . one of the crucial conditions of a peaceful development of the situations in Europe."(68) Again, Poland had failed to contain the growing power of the Federal Republic of Germany.

One of the main reasons for the repeated failure of Warsaw's supposedly independent initiatives--of which Gomulka's was to be the last--was Poland's strict adherence to the Soviet foreign policy line. Polish government propaganda maintained that the governments of Central Europe all had a common security interest and that the small powers had an opportunity to act independently of the superpowers. In fact, it was no secret that Poland was attempting to advance Soviet political and military goals in Europe. In the event any of its proposals succeeded, Poland's only gains would be derived from the enhancement of Soviet security.

By the end of 1964, Poland had to abandon its former approach to European security and disarmament. From the previous emphasis on the role of small powers and partial solutions, Poland switched to the support of broad multilateral negotiations. During the XIXth session of the United Nations General Assembly, Rapacki endorsed the Soviet position by stressing a need for resolving the "problem of European security in its entirety." He continued:

> In our considered opinion, the advisability of
> convening a conference of all European states, with
> the participation, of course, of both the Soviet Union
> and the United States, should be closely examined. If
> it is deemed useful, such a conference could be
> initially prepared by representatives appointed by the
> Warsaw Treaty and NATO, and possibly, if so desired,
> by representatives sent on behalf of European states
> not belonging to the two groupings. (69)

There were two probable reasons for this shift in emphasis. The Polish government had no doubt become discouraged by the repeated rejection of its proposals and by an emphasis on discipline and unity within the bloc.

From the Soviet point of view it was no longer desirable to insist on Rapacki or even Gomulka Plans when France set an example for dismantling the policy of blocs in Europe and was demonstrating political and military self-reliance. The countries of Eastern Europe became exposed to another danger; after nearly twenty years of hesitation, the United States had made its first positive approaches to the Communist regimes. Stressing the ideological and economic weakness of the Soviet system, the American administration introduced a policy of "peaceful engagement" in Eastern Europe,(70) which was followed by a more explicitly elaborated idea of "building bridges" between the United States and the East European countries.(71) President Johnson vowed to respect the territorial status quo in Europe (it was not to be a formal recognition of the Oder-Neisse Line), and offered trade relations, cultural exchanges and increased tourism. West German politicians, meantime, argued that Bonn had the opportunity to lure the East European regimes to accept economic aid and, after German recognition of Oder-Neisse and the post-war border with Czechoslovakia, the Communists themselves might prove helpful in the task of German reunification.

To the ever-suspicious Russians, it looked like a plot organized by the "imperialists" to undermine the foundations of the Soviet bloc. Consequently, the Soviet Union felt it mandatory to make the existing division of Europe as clear and as sharp as possible.

Another challenge to the integrity of the bloc came from China, along with its European ally Albania. The attack on this occasion was from the left; for the Chinese Communists, Moscow was not radical enough. The Russians knew that the political model elaborated in China could never be an attraction for the East European allies, but Peking's calls for their national independence could.

No doubt the Brezhniev-Kosygin leadership in Moscow, whose first task was to undo Khrushchev's reforms, had decided to act quickly to strengthen the alliance. Following Poland's endorsement of a European Security Conference, East Germany was given to set out the Warsaw Pact's conditions West Germany's formal renunciation of nuclear ambitions, recognition of the German Democratic Republic, acceptance of Oder-Neisse, abandonment of all territorial claims and full normalization of political and economic relations among all European states.(72) Moscow then convened the Political Consultative Committee of the Warsaw Pact in Bucharest where East European leaders were asked to endorse a multilateral approach to NATO. The Soviets managed to achieve greater centralization of their bloc, but they failed to induce Romania to conformism. The Romanian Communists, conscious of their domestic strength, were holding out against the Soviet demands and even sent an official delegation to China for an "exchange of experience."(73) Romanian "deviation" came out into the open.

Poland, on the other hand, found itself among the most loyal supporters of the Soviet Union. For almost a decade Poland had pursued its semi-independent policy aimed at gaining Western recognition of the Oder-Neisse Line and sheltering Central Europe from the Soviet-American rivalry. Its efforts were without visible success. The last evidence of Polish futility had been the visit to France of Premier Jozef Cyrankiewicz in September, 1965. He accomplished nothing, since President de Gaulle was unwilling to confer official recognition on Oder-Neisse behind the back of West Germany.

So Warsaw went eagerly under the Soviet wing. For the first time since 1956 Poland joined in a frontal attack on the American role in Europe. "A direct peril to peace in Europe," the bloc said in the Bucharest Declaration, ". . . is posed by the present policy of the United States of America." Europe, the Warsaw Pact countries said, was not divided at Potsdam, but as a result of the policy "promoted by the U.S.A. . . . (and) based on a coalition with the militaristic and revanchist forces in West Germany."(74)

Furthermore, the United States was portrayed as a foreign power on the European continent. Washington had been acting "in the name . . . of aims which are alien to the genuine interests of the security of European peoples." The Soviet bloc advised the West European states to emulate France, since:

. . . by the joint efforts of the European states, of all social forces campaigning for peace-irrespective of their ideological, religious or other concepts-the problem of European security can be solved. The quicker the influence of the forces wishing to increase tension in the relations between European states is paralyzed, the more successfully will this task be carried out. (75)

Moscow hoped that American involvement in Vietnam would provide the possibility of isolating the United States from its European allies. Accordingly, the Communists argued that "the aim of U.S. policy in Europe had nothing in common with the vital interests of the European peoples." The time had come, members of the Soviet bloc said, for "liquidation of the military organizations both of the North Atlantic Pact and of the Warsaw Pact . . ."(76)

Poland contributed to the establishment of a tightly controlled team of Communist leaders whose role was defined by Moscow. The period of relative "democratization within the bloc was at an end and the new pattern of relations within the bloc contained features reminiscent of Cominform. Once more, the countries of Eastern Europe were firmly under Moscow's thumb.

President de Gaulle's visit to Warsaw in September, 1967, proved how resistant the Soviet bloc had become to Western political temptations. With the establishment of the Fifth Republic in 1958, France moved to challenge the policy of blocs in Europe by eroding American influence. By the mid-1960s, after the liquidation of the Algerian War, President de Gaulle blocked political and economic integration of Western Europe, and opposed the notion of a unified Germany as well as any nuclear ambitions Bonn might nurture.

As long as France focused on harming American interests in Europe, Moscow was a delighted onlooker. When General de Gaulle looked eastward, which is what he did when his initial quest for support failed to attract the West Europeans, it was another matter. France was considering a kind of Versailles arrangement in the East, a logical move, it seemed, since French power was being eclipsed not only by the United States but by an emerging West Germany. France needed not only to strengthen its own nuclear "force de frappe" as a military deterrent and political stick, but to encourage the Communist regimes of the Soviet bloc to follow its example of self-assertion. At that point, the French ceased to play into Soviet hands and the impact of Gaullist policies had to be contained.

In Poland, however, the political views of General de Gaulle received a friendly reception, but not without official propaganda having to perform some vigorous gymnastics. The relative economic weakness of France, for example, was dis- counted since it would be a serious oversimplification to insist upon the "one-sided influence of economics upon superstructure." De Gaulle's intense nationalism was described as patriotism--a positive feeling--and admired, while his anti-communism was sidestepped by noting that de Gaulle himself had argued that political regimes were passing phenomena because nations were the only "indestructible" elements. Altogether the Polish interpretation of French nationalism seemed to be following Lenin's dictum that everything must be regarded as ideologically correct as long as it served the interests of the Commu- nists.(77)

The Polish regime had a genuine interest in supporting France. President de Gaulle was the first Western leader willing to assign an Eastern European country an important role in Europe.

During his visit, de Gaulle flattered Poland as a "popular, solid, respectable and powerful reality" and extended an impli- cit invitation to the Poles to take their distance from the Soviet Union, to adopt, as he put it, "wider horizons," and to follow, as France was doing a "new vocation that is far-flung." The French leader seemed to be offering to revive the old Paris- Warsaw entente. The goal of his trip, he said, was to "spot- light a capital fact for Europe: the solidarity between France and Poland which never ceased even when it was in eclipse." Clearly he did not expect Poland to sever its political and military ties with Moscow--but he would welcome it if the Poles, a part of what he delineated as "Central Europe" as distinct from "Eastern Europe," would somehow curtail Soviet influence. De Gaulle pleased the Poles by stating that Poland's borders with East Germany "are and must stay where they are now," but the explicit French support for Oder-Neisse was conspicuously missing from the final communique.(78)

In any event, Gomulka resisted the temptation. He candidly recalled that the pre-war Franco-Polish alliance had spared

28

neither party from "the catastrophe of defeat and Hitlerian occupation." A "renascent Poland," Gomulka said, had drawn the "fundamental conclusion," that of taking "the path of friendship and alliance with . . . the Soviet Union" and the other socialist countries of Eastern Europe. This, he said, was the "keystone" of Polish foreign policy. Because of it, "Today for the first time, France can establish friendly relations with Eastern Europe without the dilemma of choosing between Poland and her powerful Eastern neighbor." Privately he was to concede that "any weakening of these (Polish-Soviet) ties would be fatal for Poland" and he was praised by the Soviets for his political realism. In the Russian view, "de Gaulle was a megalomaniacal satrap who had lost all sense of reality because the only prestige that France had gained from his policies existed only in his imagination."(79)

Polish leaders recognized that France was politically weak and geographically distant and could not be considered seriously as an alternative guarantor of Poland's security. The Poles had forgotten neither the risks of antagonizing Russia nor the questionable reliability of Western guarantees.

As the Warsaw regime saw it, Poland's security was firmly based on three pillars: the treaty of friendship and mutual assistance with the Soviet Union (the only Great Power which recognized the Oder-Neisse Line); the bilateral treaties of friendship and mutual assistance with all the other countries of the Soviet bloc, and finally the regional system of collective security, the Warsaw Treaty Organization.

The primary task of the Warsaw Pact was to safeguard the fruits of victory over Germany as the Potsdam Agreement defined them. Such a security system had protected Poland against Germany as well as against Russia by eliminating traditional anti-Soviet elements from Polish policy. Though the system was not perfect, it had proven effective. Poland might be willing to trade it, but only for a system of collective security in Europe.

This is how the Soviet bloc countries intended to protect the status quo in Eastern Europe. For the Polish ruling elite, the concept of security was identical to the status quo and it had to include a set of conditions which the Poles officially advanced:

1. Acceptance of all international borders in Europe; including the Oder-Neisse Line and the border between East and West Germany;
2. Recognition of the existence of two German states;
3. Renunciation by the Federal Republic of Germany of any desire to gain control of nuclear weapons, directly or indirectly;
4. Recognition of West Berlin as a separate political unit not an integral part of West Germany.(80)

In addition to these requirements, the Soviet bloc demanded assurances for the incontrovertibility of Communist rule in Eastern Europe. Specifically, it wanted:

1. Legitimization of Communist control of the entire region;
2. International guarantees that this control would never be challenged from outside and that the West would never interfere when the regimes of the Soviet bloc suppressed domestic opposition.

This last point was made explicit during the Czechoslovakian crisis of 1968. Officially, Poland argued that the West German attempt at "peeling" Czechoslovakia away from the Soviet alliance had to be stopped by the use of military force, (81) but Gomulka later conceded that "nobody took seriously the possibility of any kind of aggression from the West." The real danger, as he saw it, was that the policy of liberalization in Czechoslovakia might undermine Communist power in Poland. "I told them (the Soviets) straight out," said Gomulka, "that I could give absolutely no guarantees for what might happen in my country . . . would socialism with a human force prevail.(82)

Gomulka's definition of national security therefore excluded both the Romanian deviation from the Soviet foreign policy line and the Czechoslovakian type of pluralism.

The Polish leaders in Warsaw perceive the present system in Poland to be the creature of the circumstances that developed as a consequence of the Second World War, and the international system put in place as a result of those circumstances still prevails. Their primary attention, therefore, has been concentrated on perpetuating the system that favors and acts as a warranty to their retention of power. This has been the fundamental link between the domestic reality in Poland and the foreign policy of Warsaw's Communist regime.

## Poland's *Westpolitik*

Once the 1970 Polish-German treaty was signed, Warsaw could no longer claim that West Germany was a menace. With Bonn's recognition of Oder-Neisse, Poland's frontiers became more secure. Still, one could wonder how much Poland's traditional position had really changed. The country again found itself between two superior neighbors, Russia and Germany. Soviet Russia posed certain obvious dangers because of the Brezhnev Doctrine, while fear of Germany was caused by concern about what might happen should the economic giant on the Rhine decide it no longer had to be a political dwarf.(83)

In the early 1970s, Poland entered a period of unprece- dented economic expansion, reconciliation with its neighbors and diplomatic activity. At the center of attention were Poland's ties with the Soviet Union, the two German states, the United States and France.

Reconciliation with Russia and Germany was a matter of national security. Russians and Germans had to be reassured there was no cause for apprehension about Poland and that Poland could become a useful partner and ally.

Despite initial resistance, Poland gradually accepted most of the political conditions imposed by the Soviets. A common ideology and similar security needs in Europe encouraged cooper- ation between the Warsaw regime and the Soviets. But these good relations were confined to the official level. Anti-Russian sentiments in Poland were strong; the "friendship" between the two nations was quite artificial and was in the custody of a regime which could not allow itself to question its allegiance to Moscow.

Regardless of the authenticity of Polish-Russian reconcili- ation, few had doubts about the necessity for a close alliance. It was unlikely that it could evolve into a partnership between equals, given Soviet insistence on a veto over critical Polish domestic and foreign policy decisions, but there was a trend toward an increasing measure of independence.

Moscow had learned to observe certain limits in its policy toward Poland in order to prevent outbursts of anti-Russian feeling or even domestic violence. Brezhnev, like Khrushchev before him, was reluctant to risk the use of force against Poland, while the Poles refrained from conduct that would incite Moscow to the point of military intervention. Both nations were mistrustful of one another, but each respected mutual rights.

Growing Soviet tolerance and Warsaw's ability to influence Moscow's decisions promoted a feeling of self-confidence among Polish leaders. There was a feeling that the system of which Poland was a part increased the country's international weight. As a leading Warsaw newspaper argued:

. . . the effectiveness of our policy in the West depends upon our position in the socialist system . . . In the present constellation of forces in Europe, our country is the first ally of the strongest European power--one of the world superpowers--the Soviet Union. (84)

Normalization between Poland and West Germany was more natural. The Treaty of 1970, which was preceded by important psychological changes within both nations, became a starting point for formal relations between Poland and the Federal Republic of Germany. Reconciliation, of course, required Bonn's acceptance of Germany's post-war territorial losses and a reconsideration on Poland's part of its deep suspicion of Germany. Once the normal channels were open, however, the reticence of decades was overcome. A people-to-people dialogue could begin immediately. West Germany became Poland's number two trading partner and other exchanges developed apace. But potentially the most important element in the process of normalization was the decision by both parties to revise school textbooks dealing with mutual relations. Unfair historical accounts were a great source of misinformation and prejudice.

There remained, however, one source of contention between the Poles and the Germans. Poland insisted on the settlement of the "account of wrong," that is, compensation to Polish citizens for their sufferings during the wartime years of occupation and for their underpaid labor as foreign workers in Germany. Warsaw was inspired in this case not by economic considerations alone but as a moral issue, proof that the Germans were guilty of starting the war.(85)

The West German government already had made amends to citizens of the West European states and Israel. Its reluctance to deal with the Poles was based on a West German law that prohibited such payments to individuals of countries which had no diplomatic relations with the Federal Republic before 1963. But the Poles argued that if there were no relations before 1963, it was because the West Germans declined to establish them.(86) Warsaw, incidentally, made no similar claims on the East Germans since Poland received reparations from the Soviet zone of occupation of Germany right after the war.(87)

In the broader context, of course, these were secondary concerns. Poland appeared more secure than ever. Its territory was not the object of claims by any other state, a considerable benefit to a nation constantly transferred either east or west. The Poles were able to look differently on their political role in Europe. The self-confidence this imparted is evidenced in a statement of a Polish journalist who said that:

> . . . after so many years spent in drudgery, anxiety and facing questions without answers, we can wipe the sweat off our brows and take a look around the whole of Europe with the feeling of the man who built the foundations and begins to construct his home. (88)

Poland's alliance with the Soviet Union continued to be essential and Edward Gierek, who succeeded Gomulka as party leader after the December, 1970, worker protests, left no doubt that "friendship" with Moscow must be the point of departure for

national security considerations.(89)  Close ties with the
Soviet Union, however, did not exclude Poland from taking a
broader interest in international affairs in the hope of contributing toward the dismantling of the iron curtain in Europe.
With the onset of Soviet-American detente in the early Seventies
this appeared even more practicable.

The basic logic underlying Gierek's approach toward the
Soviet Union involved the convergence of the security needs of
both countries.  Added to this was the fact of Poland's weight
as number two in the alliance, opening the possibility for
independent foreign policy initiatives without directly challenging Soviet supremacy.  Gierek's formula was to behave as a
competent and trustworthy partner of the Soviets while pushing
Polish initiatives short of the point of irritating Moscow.

Only fifteen days after taking over the party leadership,
Gierek reported to Moscow for talks with Brezhnev.  His first
task was to reassure the Soviet leadership that there was no
danger of revisionism in Poland and that the party was in firm
control after the Baltic riots.  Gierek endorsed the Soviet view
of the world situation, taking the orthodox line:  The principal
goals of Poland and the Soviet Union were said to be consolidation of the Communist movement and the struggle against
"imperialism."(90)

Later, Gierek provided some elaboration of this international platform.  The policy of detente was defined as the
continuation of the struggle with capitalism without precipi-
tating a military confrontation.  Peace among nations does not
mean peace between the classes.  As a guest at the XXIV Congress
of the Soviet Communist Party in early 1971, Gierek, in rather
submissive tones (which ousted Gomulka would not have used),
pointed to the Soviet Union as the leader of the international
Communist movement and pointed out the Soviet comrades were
carrying the main burden in the struggle with "imperialism" on a
global scale.  Speaking for Poland, Gierek reprimanded the
Chinese leadership for its anti-Soviet policy and for sabotaging
international Communist solidarity.  He demanded that Israel
return Arab lands seized in the 1967 war, condemned American
involvement in Vietnam and concluded by praising the economic
integration within COMECON and lauding the military might of the
Soviet Union.  There were no surprises.

In every respect, the positions taken by the Polish leader
were identical to those of the Soviets.  On the surface, it
appeared as absolute subordination of Polish interests.  But in
fact, Gierek was preparing the terrain for Poland's Westpolitik.

First of all, he provided timely outside support to
Brezhnev who was facing opposition in the Politburo to his
detente policy.  Second, he committed Poland to detente while
paying lip service to the ideological struggle--this was a move
designed to appease hardliners in both Communist parties.  Next,
his detailed enumeration of Poland's international objectives
was intended to reassure Soviet leaders that there were no dis-
crepancies between Poland and the Soviet Union:  Bilateral
relations between Warsaw and the countries of Western Europe and

the United States were intended to be, and should be, regarded
as extensions of Soviet foreign policy.

The renewal of confidence between Moscow and Warsaw was
combined with an added emphasis on equality, mutual consultation
and coordination.  The Soviet bloc, it was argued, should be an
example of international partnership in which roles were equit-
ably divided and a climate of respect and trust prevailed.(91)
The organization of vassals under one feudal lord was no longer
possible.  Poland must therefore have a right to elaborate and
carry out its foreign policy and the Soviet Union must follow
the same rules of procedure within the bloc as its partners did.
Thus did the pragmatic Gierek gain some degree of control over
the decisions made in Moscow, security from Soviet interference
and a green light for independent bilateral relations with the
West.

Emblematic of this changed pattern of relations was
Moscow's conclusion of a consular agreement with the Poles, a
welcome development in light of the sometimes arbitrary conduct
of Soviet officials in Poland.  In November, 1956, the status of
Soviet military units in Poland was defined, but no such code
covered Soviet civilian personnel who were beyond the reach of
the Polish authorities.  The new convention specified in detail
the reciprocal rights, obligations and immunities of all Soviets
in Poland and all Polish citizens in the Soviet Union.(92)

The Soviet leadership also was to acknowledge the principle
of collegiality and to recognize Poland's special role in the
Communist system.  Meetings between Brezhnev and Gierek became
regular occurrences.  Moscow gave the impression of making no
major foreign policy moves without first consulting two of its
allies--Poland and East Germany.  Trips by the Soviet general
secretary to Bonn or Washington were preceded by brief visits to
Warsaw and East Berlin.(93)  These were gestures of solidarity
and as reassurance that the Kremlin would not revert to
Stalinist practices of selling out Polish interests, as at
Rapallo or the Molotov-Ribbentrop pact in 1939.

Moreover, Edward Gierek and Erich Honecker, the East German
leader, gained special distinction when Brezhnev awarded them
the Order of Lenin.  For Gierek it was a reward for "outstanding
achievements in the development of friendship and cooperation"
between Poland and the Soviet Union.(94)  Another amicable
Soviet gesture toward Poland was the launching of the Polish-
Soviet satellite "Interkosmos-Kopernik 500."(95)

On a small scale, the Soviet bloc was undergoing an evolution similar to that observed in the Western alliance.  In the
East, leaders like Gierek were taking advantage of the trend
without exposing their nations to the danger of Soviet military
intervention.  Like the Polish positivists at the end of the
Nineteenth Century, Gierek was trading loyalty for freedom in
economic and cultural affairs.

Political dividends also were evident.  During the Soviet-
American negotiations in Vladivostok, for example, Brezhnev
raised no objections to improved Polish-American relations.  As
Poland's prestige grew, in and out of the bloc, so did its
chances to influence Soviet attitudes whenever Polish interests

were at stake.  The conduct of the Polish leadership was
reminiscent of the tactics used by Chancellor Adenauer, who made
West German foreign policy an extension of Washington's at a
time when the national recovery of the Federal Republic had to
be the first priority.  Adenauer's successors subsequently found
solid ground for a more independent and imaginative foreign
policy course.

Since the government of the German Democratic Republic was
pursuing essentially the same policy toward the Soviet Union as
Poland, and since both regimes had similar interests vis-a-vis
Bonn and Moscow, the formation of a Warsaw-East Berlin axis
should not have been a surprise, especially given the improved
relations between Moscow and Bonn.  The usefulness of Polish-
East German collaboration was recognized by Gomulka at the end
of the 1950s, but the development of a "Northern tier" was
scuttled by Walter Ulbricht, the East German leader, who
regarded Poland as a source of heresy in the Communist bloc.  It
was also a case of personal animosity between two men competing
for the second position in the alliance.

When the old rivals were succeeded by Edward Gierek and
Erich Honecker, a more rational arrangement emerged.  Bilateral
economic relations were given added emphasis without detracting
from the common stress on security matters.  Consultation became
standard practice.  Gierek summarized these exchanges in the
following way:

> Poland is an important link in this community and,
> moreover, it represents the immediate fallback posi-
> tion for the socialist German Democratic Republic.
> That is why there is a complete identity of interests
> and a mutual linkage of policy between our two coun-
> tries. (96)

His meaning was clear:  Poland wanted to be regarded as a
partial substitute for the Soviet Union.  With basically the
same purpose in mind, Poland adapted its Westpolitik to the
demands of the new international situation.  Warsaw promoted the
impression that its diplomats were representatives of the entire
socialist community, due to the identity of views between the
Soviet and Polish governments.  At the same time, Poland took
every possible advantage to advance its own prestige.

Poland's European strategy was inspired by the idea that it
was possible to develop a functional model of cooperation among
all the countries of Europe regardless of their political
systems.  Bilateral arrangements were to be supplements to
involvement in multilateral negotiations on a European security
system.  This pattern permitted Poland to profit from its state-
to-state contacts.  It was an opportunity to build a network of
bilateral ties with the countries of Western Europe without
putting into question the utility and purpose of military blocs.
Extensive credits and access to sophisticated technology in the
West were the most immediate gains.  But in the long run,
Poland's aim was to balance Soviet patronage with a beneficial
economic and political link to the West.

This motive soon became evident.  No doubt due to the rich
history of Poland's political and cultural relations with
France, Gierek decided to launch his new Westpolitik in Paris.
The immediate results may not have fulfilled his grand expectations, but they were nevertheless considerable.  For example,
France disappointed him by refusing Poland's request for most-
favored-nation status (it would have violated French obligations
as a member of the European Economic Community), but it did not
disappoint when it came to providing substantial credits and
trade.  And although the French would not agree to a formal
treaty of friendship and cooperation, the Joint Declaration of
Friendship and Cooperation was renewed.  Both sides vowed to
conduct regular bilateral consultations on security matters at
the foreign ministers' level.

Most important, perhaps, was the fact that the renewed
version of the Declaration went somewhat beyond the scope of
Polish-French relations.  It contained four principles of
peaceful coexistence, with each country pledging:
1.  To refrain from the use or the threat of force;
2.  To respect the sovereignty, equality and indepen-
    dence of other nations;
3.  To refrain from interference in others' internal
    affairs;
4.  To respect existing frontiers.(97)

This pattern of involvement in European politics was
applied successfully in other cases.  On the basis of principles
similar to those contained in the Franco-Polish Declaration,
Poland deepened its bilateral relations with Belgium, Italy and
the Scandinavian countries.  By limiting the political content
of these contacts to statements dealing with peaceful coexistence, Poland could safely increase its economic and cultural exchanges with the countries of Western Europe.  The net
result was the unlikelihood that Poland's leaders would ever
again agree to violate the sovereignty of another country--as in
the case of Czechoslovakia, say--since by cutting their economic
assistance and closing their markets in retaliation, the states
of Western Europe could seriously disrupt Poland's economy.

Poland also was able to improve its relations with the
United States.  Ratification of the Polish-West German Treaty
enabled the American government to proceed with its policy
toward Poland without alienating Bonn.  President Nixon agreed
to sign a declaration which stated among other things that "both
sides welcomed the treaty between Poland and the Federal Republic of Germany signed on December 7, 1970, including its border
provisions."(98)  President Nixon's arrival in Warsaw immediately after his first Moscow summit left the flattering
impression that Washington would respect Poland's claim to semi-
independent status within the Soviet bloc.

The United States seemed to have no interest in using its
influence on Poland to cause a split within the Soviet-led
alliance.  On the contrary, it was felt that improvement of
Polish-American relations should be managed without straining
Polish-Soviet ties, if only because Poland was in a position to

temper belligerent tendencies in Moscow should they reappear. Among the nations of Eastern Europe, Poland had probably developed the strongest political and economic stake in fostering the climate of detente, a development Poland's leaders wanted to make "irreversible." President Ford, President Nixon's successor, found the continuing improvement of Polish-American relations to be a useful adjunct to progress with Moscow.

The political aspects of Polish-American relations were formally confined to a mutual commitment to the principles of peaceful coexistence and to a common support for detente. More significant were the economic exchanges opened up by President Nixon. The United States made its markets and credits available by granting most-favored-nation status, and Warsaw took full advantage of these privileges. A huge deficit in the Polish balance of payments was a natural consequence of the dynamic growth in Poland's trade with a much stronger and highly developed partner. The question was how long Poland could live on American credits while declaring its full political and ideological allegiance to the rival superpower. In short time, the Polish debt to the United States rapidly rose beyond one quarter of the total annual value of trade, normally considered to be the margin of safety for a creditor as well as a prudent borrower.(99)

Still, both Washington and Warsaw continued to examine the possibilities of further expanding their trade relations. Poland's interest was evident--the United States was providing Poland with modern technology, giving it a realistic chance for modernization and increased political self-confidence. Some analysts felt that the United States also was helping to make the Communist regime in Poland politically more acceptable to the Polish people since popular economic expectations were being more nearly fulfilled.

For the United States the benefits were several. Once the Polish-West German Treaty was concluded and the border dispute was ended, Poland could be expected to help moderate hard-line Soviet foreign policy. With the Polish people coming to anticipate the attainment of Western economic standards, and with the clear dependence of this outcome on continued good relations with the capitalist world, the Polish government would return at its hazard to a policy of hostility toward the United States and Western Europe. The risks for the Warsaw regime were seen to be economic catastrophe and revolt. The trend was therefore leading to the eventuality of Poland's remaining the military ally of Moscow, but becoming the economic client and political partner of the Western capitals.

In the State Department and the Politburo of the Polish United Workers Party, officials saw no ready alternative for Poland to the policy of detente and close economic ties with the West. At the same time, neither the Polish people nor, least of all, the regime was ready to put into question the purpose or the necessity of the alliance with the Soviet Union. Washington had reason to welcome the regime's pro-Soviet posture, since it was thought to provide protection against an abrupt Soviet invasion that would not fail to jeopardize U.S. investments in

Poland. The Russians, for their part, seemed convinced that the Polish-American economic exchanges would not have adverse effects on the balance of power.

But it should be mentioned that regardless of how much unanimity Moscow was able to manufacture in military-strategic matters, the prevailing trend in Eastern Europe was toward diversity in domestic and international policy. While the United States was not necessarily interested in seeing the disintegration of Soviet influence in Eastern Europe, the United States did want to stimulate these centrifugal developments through economic means.

When foreign policy is dominated by economic matters, political dividends do not follow immediately. Both Poland and the United States were willing to wait for their future political gains: Poland hoped its greater economic strength would multiply its political influence, while the United States was content to see further liberalization from Soviet domination. In essence it came to much the same thing, a stronger more independent Poland losing interest in a one-sided alliance with the Soviet Union. So Polish-American relations acquired mutual aims: non-provocation of the Soviet Union and encouragement of economic exchanges.

The 1975 Conference on Security and Cooperation in Europe and the Mutual Balanced Force Reduction talks were two major areas of Poland's multilateral activity. But since strategic issues were involved, Poland had to act under much closer Soviet supervision. In 1969, the Communist leaders initiated a vigorous campaign to induce the other countries of Europe to convene these conferences. The Political Consultative Committee of the Warsaw Pact put forward the following pre-conditions:

1. Acceptance of the territorial status quo in Europe.
2. Recognition of the existence of two German states.
3. Invalidation of the Munich Pact.
4. FRG's renunciation of the control of nuclear weapons.
5. Recognition of West Berlin as a separate international entity.(100)

Three years later, the first four conditions were met and sufficient compromise was reached on the Berlin issue to warrant the convening of the European conferences. Poland had assumed an active role, particularly on behalf of the conference on security and cooperation, since its best hope for desatellization, economic prosperity and national cultural development was based on the liquidation of the effects of the Cold War. Poland had several compelling reasons for supporting the idea of collective security in Europe.

The Poles were opposed to the notion of an "Atlantic Europe." Political and economic consolidation of Western Europe would exclude the countries of Central Europe from the Western world, and many feared that the consequences of such a division would be as severe as the split of Christianity into Eastern and

Western churches.  Poland feared separation from Western culture and technology.

In political terms, the Atlantic conception implied that peace in Europe would continue to be based on the balance of power principle.  Nothing would be changed regarding Poland's strategic situation.  The country would still be squeezed between two superior powers (the United States of Europe and the Soviet Union) and its high degree of adherence to Soviet foreign policy could not be modified.

Some analysts went even farther to argue that a united Western Europe--the third superpower--would constitute a direct menace to Poland.  These analysts pointed to the expansionist tradition of West European nations and said that Western Europe's emancipation from American tutelage would encourage a United States of Europe to satisfy any expansionist desires at the expense of Central Europe.(101)

Moreover, many Warsaw politicians were of the opinion that sooner or later a united Western Europe would fall under the domination of West Germany.  With equally great apprehension, Poland observed the normalization of relations between Bonn and Peking, noting that China was the only big power interested in promoting German unification.  The Chinese encouraged the West Europeans to consolidate their alliance in the hopes of seeing another superpower threaten Russia from the West.(102)  The Poles suspected that West German hard-liners, such as Franz-Josef Strauss, were considering an alliance similar to Hitler's with Japan.  In the case of China, such an arrangement could become even more dangerous since it would involve one of the most technologically advanced countries in the world with the most populated country in the world--a combination which would make the Russians even more insecure and intractable.

Poland backed Soviet opposition to the Western alliance. Its views invariably were couched in terms of sovereignty and territorial integrity.  According to Communist observers, NATO (or the Common Market) violated the principle of national self-determination and further integration increased the danger of war.(103)  Neither Russia nor Poland were looking for a new superpower on its western threshold, and each argued that West European unity was a relic of the Cold War.  But actually Poland's dilemma was clear:  Disintegration of the European community might free Germany from supranational constraints, yet a strong and cohesive community raised the spectre of collective West European expansionism.  The best solution was to resist complete West European integration while preventing fragmentation and neutrality.

Another Polish aim was to gain a permanent legitimization of Communist rule in Poland and of the Oder-Neisse Line. Although nobody was questioning the authority of the Communist regimes in Central Europe--they were recognized by the Western powers--there were nonetheless considerable doubts about their ability to command respect among their own people without Soviet backing.  Nor until a European security system was established could the Communist regime in Poland claim that its domestic and international authority had both legal and full political support in Moscow and Washington. The same could be said about the Oder-Neisse Line, which could not become "final" in the strict legal sense until it was recognized in a multilateral treaty signed by the four principal victors of the Second World War.

Also, the Polish government felt that a reduction in East-West tensions would bring about at least a partial withdrawal of the United States from Europe. If the high level of Soviet involvement in Central Europe was due to concern about the American presence in Western Europe, Moscow's sensitivity toward its western flank would diminish once a less threatening power configuration was arranged. As a consequence, the Poles expected a wider margin of Soviet tolerance in Central Europe. Reduction of Russian anxiety about the western flank might put an end to the satellization of Central Europe.

But a reduction of the American role in Europe could have a contrary effect and the Poles were fully aware of its dangers. Once a multilateral agreement--instead of a balance of power-- defined international politics in Europe, its Western segment would become the prey of Russia. An old Bolshevik dream of carrying communism to the Atlantic never entirely vanished, and it would finally be given a chance for success.(104) Poland's fate in such circumstances might recall the events of August and September, 1939. It is, therefore, in Poland's best interest to see that Soviet power in Europe is always balanced in the West.

The Helsinki Accord which concluded the conference met Poland's expectations, since it was a meeting of two alliances guided by the principle of status quo. Unlike conferences in Vienna (1815), Versailles (1919), and Yalta (1945), the meeting in Helsinki created no new situation in Europe, but only acknowledged the existing configuration of forces, including the political-military texture of the Soviet bloc.

The Accord, however, endorsed several rules of international law and politics as binding all parties in their intra and inter bloc relations. This provided some limited comfort to smaller states like Poland. These principles included sovereignty, non use of force, territorial integrity, noninterference into domestic affairs, respect for human rights, equality of all states, cooperation, and recognition of all existing borders in Europe as permanent. New atmosphere in Europe has been created and higher moral standards attached to Soviet behavior, but no tangible political or military barrier has been imposed on the Soviet ability and determination to enforce the Brezhniev doctrine against their satellites in Eastern Europe. This self-proclaimed Soviet right to police Poland and other neighbors was explicitly included in Soviet interpretation of the Helsinki Accord, which stresses principles of sovereignty and noninterference into domestic affairs in such a way that the notorious Soviet "fraternal help" rendered on "invitation" does not constitute a breach of international law.

To make this imperial Soviet right explicitly clear, immediately following the Conference the principle of priority of Soviet interest over national preferences has found recognition in the domestic laws of the East European countries. In

the case of Poland, a 1976 constitutional amendment elevated
"friendship and cooperation with the USSR and other socialist
states" to the supreme law of the land.  A Polish attempt in
1981 to depart from Soviet criteria of a socialist state was
defined in Moscow as "incompatible with the Constitution of the
Polish People's Republic into which the principle of strengthening friendship with the USSR was written."

It is the Brezhniev doctrine written into the domestic law
which subordinated the national interest of Poland and other
nations under the Soviet domination to the interest of the
"socialist commonwealth" where the defense of Communism "is the
common affair" of all countries involved.

The Soviets also advance moral claims to justify their
demand of loyalty from the Poles, since the Polish people owe
their freedom to the "hundreds of thousands" of Russians who
sacrificed their lives in the struggle to liberate Poland from
the Nazis.  And now, the Soviets insist that Polish statehood
continues to be protected by "units of the Red Army standing
guard on the Western borders of the socialist commonwealth, of
which the Polish People's Republic is also a part."(105)  The
protection of the Polish statehood from the Soviet invasion
became the principal motive for imposition of martial law in
December 1981.  Communist system in Poland continues to be the
key guarantee of national security, and the leaders of Poland,
like the leaders of Russia during the Mongolian domination, are
prepared to suppress their own people to deprive the Russians of
an excuse for invasion.

Notes

1. Zygmunt Wojciechowski, "Poland and Germany, Ten Centuries of Struggle," in Zygmunt Wojciechowski (ed.), Poland's Place in Europe (Poznan: Institut Zachodni, 1947), p. 265.

2. Piotr S. Wandycz, Soviet-Polish Relations, 1917-1921 (Cambridge, Mass.: Harvard University Press, 1968), p. 15.

3. Documents on Polish-Soviet Relations, 1939-1945, vol. I (London-Melbourne-Toronto: Heinemann, General Sikorski Institute, 1961), p. 65. Hereafter cited as DPSR.

4. S. Konovalev, Russo-Polish Relations. A Historical Survey, Princeton, N.J.: Princeton University Press, 1945), p. 17.

5. Jedrzej Giertych, Politika Polska w Dziejach Europy (London: Nakladem Autora, 1947), p. 541.

6. The New York Times, August 17, 1945.

7. Jozef Beck, Final Report (New York: Robert Speller and Sons Publishers, Inc., 1957), p. 272.

8. DPSR, vol. I, p. 65.

9. The Liquidation of Poland, Voluntary or Compulsory And by Whose Authority? (Glasgow: P. Donegan and Co., Ltd., 1945), p. 11.

10. DPSR, vol. I, p. 65.

11. Maria Turlejska, Spor o Polske (Warszawa: Ksiazka i Wiedza, 1970), p. 36.

12. DPSR, vol. I, p. 265.

13. DPSR, vol. I, p. 285.

14. The New York Times, April 20, 1943.

15. Piotr S. Wandycz, Czechoslovak-Polish Confederation and the Great Powers, 1940-43 (Indiana University Publications, Slavic and East European Series, vol. s, 1956), p. 39.

16. Ibid., p. 92.

17. Manifesto of the Committee of National Liberation (the founding document of the post-war Poland in Podstawy Nauk

42

Politicznych, Dokumenty i Materialy vol. I, 2nd edition (Warszawa: Ksiazka i Wiedza, 1972), pp. 236-45.

18. Oscar Lange, "Rola Polski w Powojennym Swiecie," in: Na Progu Wolnosci (London:  Polish Progressive Club, 1944), pp. 2-3.

19. Oscar Lange, "Poland's Foreign Policy," Poland of Today, March 1946, pp. 4-5.

20. Stanislaw Mikolajczyk, "The Polish Government and the Future of Poland," Polish Review, September 13, 1944, p. 2.

21. DPSR, vol. II, p. 417.

22. The New York Times, February 21, 1945.

23. Khrushchev Remembers, The Last Testament (Boston: Little, Brown and Company, 1974), p. 171.

24. The New York Times, June 1, 1945.

25. The New York Times, December 31, 1945.

26. The New York Times, February 1, 1946.

27. Arthur Bliss Lane, I Saw Poland Betrayed (New York:  The Bobbs-Merrill Company, 1948), p. 279.

28. Wlodzimierz T. Kowalski, Polityka Zagraniczna RP 1944-1947 (Warszawa:  Polski Instytut Spraw Miedzynarodowych, 1971), pp. 19-20.

29. Polska Ludowa--Zwiazek Radziecki, 1944-1974. Zbior Dokumentow i Materialow (Warszawa, 1974), pp. 57-60).

30. Dziennik Ustaw 1947, No. 35, p. 167.

31. Rzeczpospolita, August 27, 1945.

32. The New York Times, March 6, 1946.

33. Pravda, February 8 and 11, 1946.

34. Friedrich von Wilpert, The Oder-Neisse Problem (New York: Atlantic-Forum, 1969), p. 57.

35. Rzeczpospolita, June 3, 1946.

36. Polish official quoted in The New York Times, September 18, 1946.

37. Kowalski, op. cit., p. 108.

38. Jozef Swiatlo, <u>Za Kulisami Bezpieki i Partii</u> (No publisher, 1954), p. 39.

39. The <u>New York Times</u>, January 19, 1947.

40. The <u>New York Times</u>, December 7, 1947.

41. <u>Rzeczpospolita</u>, February 14, 1947.

42. Kowalski, <u>op. cit.</u>, pp. 335-340.

43. Stephen Horak (ed.), <u>Poland's International Affairs, 1919-1960</u> (Bloomington: Indiana University, 1964), pp. 185-186.

44. <u>Ibid.</u>, pp. 188-189.

45. <u>Ibid.</u>, pp. 190-191.

46. <u>Ibid.</u>, pp. 194 and 196-197.

47. The <u>New York Times</u>, November 9 and 11, 1949.

48. <u>Khrushchev Remembers, The Last Testament, op. cit.</u>, p. 176.

49. W. W. Kulski, "Central Europe in Transition," <u>Journal of Central European Affairs</u>, No. 4 (1949), p. 363.

50. The <u>New York Times</u>, May 28, 1949.

51. Horak, <u>op. cit.</u>, p. 201. See also, Manfred Lachs, "Konferencja Warszawska," <u>Nowe Drogi</u>, No. 5 (1955), pp. 3-10.

52. Wlodzimierz Wieczorek, "Historyczny Rozwoj Idei Bezpieczenstwa Europejskiego," <u>Sprawy Miedzynarodowe</u>, No. 9 (1970), p. 65.

53. Jozef Winiewicz, "Speech at the U.N. General Assembly," October 10, 1966; in <u>Polish Viewpoint, Disarmament, Denuclearization, European Security Documents, Declarations, Statements</u> (Warsaw: "Polonia" Publishing House, 1967), p. 68.

54. "The Polish Government Memorandum Concerning the Creation of an Atom-Free Zone in Central Europe," in <u>Polish Viewpoint</u> . . ., <u>op. cit.</u>, p. 4

55. Andrzej Skowronski, "Problemy Bezpieczenstwa Zbiorowego w Europie," <u>Sprawy Miedzynarodowe</u>, Nos. 7-8 (1965), p. 23.

56. <u>Ibid.</u>, pp. 24-25.

44

57. Trybuna Ludu, March 19, 1958.

58. "The Polish Government Memorandum . . ." op. cit., p. 3.

59. Pierre Hassner, "Change and Security in Europe, Part II: In Search of a System," Adelphi Papers, No. 49 (June 1968), p. 1.

60. Bulletin des Presse und Informationsamtes der Bundesregierung 1958, No. 16, p. 131.

61. Pravda, January 11, 1958.

62. Quoted in Andrzej Lesniewski (ed.) Western Frontier of Poland, (Warsaw: Polish Institute of International Affairs, 1965), p. 140.

68. Raymond Aron, Peace and War (London: Weidenfield and Nicolson, 1966), pp. 502-503.

64. March 14, 1963.

65. Trybuna Ludu, December 28, 1963.

66. Zbiegniew K. Brzezinski, Alternative to Partition (New York: McGraw-Hill Book Company, 1965), p. 87.

67. Skowronski, op. cit., pp. 132-133.

68. Polish Viewpoint . . ., op. cit., p. 29.

69. Ibid., p. 36.

70. Zbiegniew Brzezinski and William E. Griffith, "Peaceful Engagement in Eastern Europe," Foreign Affairs, No. 4 (July 1962), pp. 642 and following.

71. The New York Times, May 24, 1964.

72. Neues Deutschland, January 23, 1966.

73. The New York Times, July 7, 1966.

74. Polish Viewpoint . . ., op. cit., p. 53.

75. Ibid., p. 54.

76. Ibid., pp. 51 and 56.

77. Zygmunt Szymanski, "O Filozofii Politycznej de Gaulle'a," Sprawy Miedzynarodowe, No. 6 (1967), p. 7.

78. "Po Wizycie de Gaulle'a, Proba Bilansu," Sprawy Miedzynarodowe, No. 10 (1967), p. 7.

79. Ignacy Szenfeld, "The Reminiscences of Wladislaw Gomulka", (Published by Radio Liberty, 1975), p. 11.

80. Alfons Klafkowski, "Uklad Polska-NRF o Podstawach Normalizacji Stosunkow Jako Element Uznania Status Quo w Europie," Sprawy Miedzynarodowe, No. 9 (1971), pp. 9-12.

81. Ignacy Krasicki, "Status Quo i Bezpiecznstwo Europejskie," Sprawy Miedzynarodowe, No. 11 (1968), p. 15.

82. Szenfeld, op. cit., p. 17.

83. Marian Podkowinski, "Olbrzym czy Karzel?" Perspektywy, January 31, 1975.

84. Ignacy Krasicki, "Nasze Miejsce w Sojuszu," Zycie Warszawy, January 22, 1971.

85. Trybuna Ludu, March 17, 1973.

86. Marian Podkowinski, "Wymowne Milczenie," Perspektywy, March 21, 1975.

87. The real obstacle to payment appeared to be the price West Germany should pay. Poland originally was insisting on a sum of 10 billion DM at a time when Chancellor Willy Brandt was willing to consider 4 billion DM. Helmut Schmidt, Brandt's successor, initially refused to consider making any payment at all, to which Poland reacted by restricting the flow of immigration to West Germany. Bonn then made another offer of 1.5 billion DM which the Poles accepted.
Information provided by the Polish officials.

88. Quoted in The New York Times, July 19, 1972.

89. VI Zjazd Polskiej Zjednoczonej Partii Robotniczej (December 6-7, 1971), in Podstawowe Materialy i Dokumenty (Warszawa, 1972), pp. 146-155.

90. Trybuna Ludu, January 6, 1971.

91. Trybuna Ludu, August 3, 1971.

92. Polska Ludowa--Zwiazek Radziecki . . ., op. cit., pp. 510-526.

93. Trybuna Ludu, May 12, 1973.

94. Pravda, June 1, 1973.

46

95. Trybuna Ludu, April 20, 1973.

96. Quoted in The New York Times, June 20, 1973.

97. Eugeniusz Gajda, Polska Polityka Zagraniczna, 1944-1974
(Warszawa: Ministerstwo Obrony Narodowej, 1974), p. 280.

98. Quoted in The New York Times, June 2, 1972.

99. Wlodzimierz Wowczuk, "Instrument Przyspieszania,"
Perspektywy, April 4, 1974.

100. Jozef Wiejacz, "Nowy Etap Tworzenia Trwalego
Bezpieczenstwa w Europie," Sprawy Miedzynarodowe, Nos.
7-8 (1973), p. 10.

101. Andrzej Towpik, "O Ogolnoeuropejskim Systemie
Bezpieczenstwa," Sprawy Miedzynarodowe, No. 1 (1972), p.
13.

102. Andrzej Janicki, "Chiny a Europa," Perspektywy, February
7, 1975.

103. "European Security: Content and Ways of Ensuring It,"
International Affairs (Moscow), November, 1971, p. 69.

104. Leo Labedz, "Detente or Deception," East-West Digest, No.
16 (1974), p. 612.

105. Note of the Central Committee of the Communist Party of
the Soviet Union and Soviet Government to the Central
Committee of the Polish United Workers Party and the
Polish Government in The New York Times, September 19,
1981.

# 2
# Territorial Integrity

## The Curzon Line

The territorial ambitions were at the heart of the Nazi and Soviet attacks on Poland in September, 1939. Hitler wanted to eliminate the corridor linking Poland with the Baltic Sea, while for Stalin the Soviet invasion was the fulfillment of a "sacred duty" to assist "brother Ukranians and White Russians inhabiting Poland" (1) by recovering the land they claimed. It was natural that Poland's future territorial configuration would emerge as a major political issue during the Second World War.

As Poland's chief international sponsor, Great Britain was the first to take a position on the issue. But while the British were skillful in appealing to Polish national pride and romanticism, they never really committed themselves to more than a guarantee of Poland's post-war independence. Britain did not indicate what independent Poland's frontiers should be. Typically, at the time of the Nazi attack on the Soviet Union in 1941, the British government declared that:

> We have not at any time adopted, since the war broke out, the line that nothing could be changed in the territorial structure of various countries. On the other hand, we do not propose to recognize any territorial changes which take place during the war, unless they take place with the free consent and good will of the parties concerned. (2)

The first real opportunity to deal with the question of Poland's eastern frontier developed under strong British pressure when General Wladislaw Sikorski, head of the Polish government in exile in London, accepted a Soviet invitation to negotiate. After several meetings with Ivan M. Maisky, the Soviet ambassador to Great Britain, a Polish-Soviet agreement was concluded on July 30, 1941.

Of special importance was the provision of the agreement in which the Soviet side recognized that the pre-war Nazi-Soviet

treaties regarding territorial changes had "lost their vali-
dity." But much was left vague.

Ambassador Maisky pointed out that "the general position of
the Soviet government as regards the Polish state was that it
maintained the point of view previously expressed in favor of
the independence of the Polish state within the limits of Polish
nationality."(3) Ambassador Maisky added that he "only wished
to state his government's point of view about the future limits
of the Polish state and did not ask the Polish government to
agree."(4) Thus, what Maisky seemed to be saying was that while
Russia would prefer Poland's eastern frontier to be the Curzon
Line--hence the reference to "the limits of Polish nationality"--it was not prepared to insist on it.

Sikorski's immediate reaction was that "the Polish government could not accept" such a solution, and in any event preferred to set aside the question of frontiers until the war was
over.(5) Sikorski's understanding of the treaty and of Polish
possibilities was much more ambitious than the Curzon Line would
have allowed. Up to the time of the Soviet victory at
Stalingrad, the prevailing view in the West was that Russia
would be defeated by Germany and that the Western coalition
would then force the Germans to capitulate. In this view, the
over-all pattern of the First World War would be repeated,
producing favorable circumstances for Poland to dictate territorial conditions to both Germany and Russia.

The British attitude toward the Polish-Russian dispute was
based on practical considerations: preservation of relative
harmony among members of the anti-Nazi coalition as well as
recognition of the reality created by Soviet occupation of the
Polish eastern territories in September, 1939. London did not
insist on an immediate solution to the Polish-Russian territorial quarrel and, like Sikorski, was willing to wait until the
end of the war.

From a strictly legal point of view, the British government
did "not recognize any territorial changes which have been
effected in Poland since August, 1939."(6) At the same time,
Anthony Eden, the Secretary of State for Foreign Affairs, told
the House of Commons that the government's position did "not
involve any guarantee of frontiers."(7) One may conclude that
as early as 1941 the differences between the Soviet and British
positions were largely academic.

The United States government was alone in backing General
Sikorski's interpretation of the Polish-Soviet understanding.
But even Washington was to relent. The State Department, after
some reflection, notified the Polish ambassador in Washington
that "in view of the successful conclusion of the treaty and its
favorable terms to both sides, the previous guarantee given by
the State Department is superfluous."(8)

Thus even at the time of Russia's maximum military indis-
position, in 1941, there was no state willing to endorse
Poland's territorial claims in the East. Accordingly, the
decision of the Polish government in London to build a domestic
consensus and to formulate a foreign policy on a deliberate

misinterpretation of the Great Powers' position was bound to fail, unless a 'miracle' was forthcoming.

The domestic aspects of the territorial controversy were of considerable importance for both Poland and Russia. Sikorski and Stalin needed all the arguments they could muster to help mobilize every individual in the fight against Nazi Germany. With patriotic feelings thus aroused, neither leader felt he could afford to pursue any policy which might affront national pride.

General Sikorski noted that "he could not accept any departure from the status which existed prior to August, 1939. He would never be able to return to his country, once having agreed to a diminished Poland."(9) Sikorski felt that only a Jagiellonian outline for Poland would be acceptable to the majority of his countrymen. No alternative would be satisfactory, because in no other way could genuine independence from Poland's neighbors be secured.

The outlook for the resolution of such a dilemma through a joint Polish-Soviet agreement was never favorable, especially since Polish and Russian national interests, as each side defined them, appeared to be mutually exclusive. A Jagiellonian Poland would have to be reconstructed at the expense of the Russians, insuring its unacceptability to Moscow in the best of circumstances. Inasmuch as the domestic prestige of the Soviet regime was in decline at the start of the war, Stalin could not be seen by his countrymen to yield to Polish territorial demands. As reported by Jan Ciechanowski, the Polish ambassador to the United States, even the "Russian (emigre) circles in the U.S.A. (particularly Kerensky's group, as well as the Ukranians and Lithuanians) started action against the return to the pre-World War II status."(10)

There is an interesting resemblance between the vulnerability of the tsarist regime during the First World War and the Soviet regime just after the Nazi onslaught. At home, the toll of collectivization and the purges had sapped the popularity of the Soviets, while Communists abroad were discredited by the Ribbentrop-Molotov pact. In contrast to Tsar Nikolai, Stalin had a perfect understanding of reality. He had no illusions and he had much better luck.

But how could he be expected to carry almost the entire burden of the war against Germany, struggle for consensus at home and simultaneously deal with the territorial issues to which all Russians were so sensitive?

During Sikorski's visit to Moscow in December, 1941, Stalin appeared willing to accept a genuine and lasting Polish-Russian reconciliation. The conclusion of General Sikorski's visit was marked by an official declaration of Friendship and Mutual Assistance. Among the declaration's most important provisions was that the Poles would fight "shoulder to shoulder with Soviet troops." The document was endorsed by Stalin, who, in an unmistakable allusion to the Ribbentrop-Molotov pact, noted that it would be "the first time that a declaration has been signed by Stalin and not by Molotov. He also added:

> Twice you have conquered Moscow in the past, and the
> Russians have been several times in Warsaw. We have
> fought each other continually. It is about time to
> finish this brawl. (11)

The issue of the future Polish-Soviet frontier was not the
subject of formal negotiations during the Sikorski visit.
Stalin, however, wanted the problem settled and made several
attempts to bring Sikorski to discuss it. Notes from the visit
indicate that Stalin at first stated that Lwow (Lvov) was a
Polish city. A moment later, he modified his statement, saying
the Poles should expect to "have a dispute about it, not with
the Russians but with the Ukrainians." He also informed his
guests that they should not count too much on British and
American aid. "We should settle our common frontier between
ourselves, and before the Peace Conference . . . Don't worry, we
will not harm you." Sikorski made it clear that he wanted to
postpone these negotiations.(12) In his last effort, Stalin
addressed Sikorski personally, going so far as to say he wanted
to change the border "chut-chut" (a little bit).(13)

Once again, Sikorski disagreed. His position was that such
a problem could be settled only by the Polish parliament. But
in fact he wanted more. He thought time was working for him and
that he would be able to secure Western support for Polish
territorial claims in the East and Soviet backing for the idea
of Polish expansion in the West.(14) As did most Polish politicians of his day, Sikorski operated on the unrealistic and
outdated concept of a multinational Poland and looked upon the
Polish-Russian demarcation line as the "frontier of Western and
Christian civilization."(15)

Stalin was shrewd enough to foresee that the Western allies
would pay no more than lip service to Poland's interests.
Though the allies might grant political asylum to Polish refu-
gees, they would not risk serious troubles with the Russians
over Poland. Were there any doubts, they were removed by the
behavior of the British and American governments during the controversy over the Katyn massacre. It appeared there was no
issue related to Poland that could separate the allies from
Soviet Russia.

In the background, the Soviet military fortunes underwent a
considerable improvement. After the Soviet victory at Stalingrad in early 1943 and the successful Kursk offensive of the
following summer, the defensive capacities of the Wehrmacht were
not sufficient to prevent the Red Army from moving westward with
almost the same speed as the Germans had advanced eastward
during their blitzkrieg in 1941. Simultaneously, Soviet dependence on military supplies from Great Britain and America diminished due to the ability of the Russians to develop their own
armaments industries east of the Urals.

Stalin's assessment of the British and American attitudes
toward the fate of the Polish government in exile was again to
be proved correct at the Moscow Conference of Foreign Ministers
in October, 1943. There, the most the Western leaders had to
say was: The United States "hope(d) the two neighbors would be

able to establish normal and friendly relations," while His
Majesty's government stated it "was prepared to make any contribution which would be found possible looking toward the re-
establishment of friendly relations between the Soviet Union and
Poland."(16)

A month later the first conference of the Big Three took
place in Tehran. Churchill was the first to inquire about
Stalin's willingness to consider the Polish issue. Stalin
declined, saying that he "had not yet felt the necessity nor the
desirability of discussing the Polish question."(17) Unlike at
the beginning of the Soviet-German war, an early settlement of
the Polish issue, including the question of Poland's eastern
frontiers, was no longer of urgent interest to the Soviets.
Now, time was working for them.(18) Prolongation of the Polish-
Soviet territorial controversy was a convenient pretext for the
continuing non-recognition of the Polish government in London
(with which it had suspended relations in April, 1943, over the
Katyn disclosures) and it provided Moscow with sufficient time
for building up rival Polish political and military establish-
ments in Russia.

If Stalin had anything to fear, it was that under British
pressure the London Poles would agree to accept Soviet territorial demands, thereby disposing of the principal cause of
Polish-Soviet disagreement. If such a development took place,
the failure of Stalin to restore recognition to the London Poles
would manifest his lack of good will, while any Soviet recognition of the Polish government in London would amount to
handing back to Churchill control over Poland's political
future. By the end of 1943, the Soviet leaders knew they could
deal unilaterally with Poland and it was Churchill who was
insisting on bilateral agreement.

The time came to pay for the political miscalculations of
1941-1943. At the outset of the Soviet-German conflict, the
West had preferred to stay on the sidelines, expecting Russia
and Germany would exhaust themselves, with the result, Churchill
hoped, that British influence would be strengthened in both Asia
and Europe. So confident of this outcome was Churchill that he
demanded no concessions from the Soviets in exchange for desper-
ately needed military supplies. To seek concessions, he felt,
would only prolong Soviet resistance. As Russia's vulnerability
decreased, the Allies discovered that the time for extracting
concessions from Stalin had elapsed. Poland was the first to
pay for this oversight.(19)

At Tehran, despite Stalin's initial "reluctance," there was
a provisional settlement of the Polish question which provided a
double advantage for him since he obtained recognition of Soviet
territorial claims in a secret "gentlemen's agreement" and was
able to do so without assuming an obligation to restore diplomatic relations with the London Poles.

Stalin didn't encounter much opposition, at least not on
the part of the Americans. Roosevelt told Stalin he, too, had
his trouble with the Poles. He told the Soviet leader that the
U.S. presidential elections were just a year away and that
"there were in the United States from six to seven million

Americans of Polish extraction and as a practical man he did not
wish to lose their vote."(20)  So whatever was agreed about
Poland at the end of the 1943 was not to be made public at least
until November, 1944, when Roosevelt would have won his fourth
term.  By that time the Red Army would be in Poland.

At Tehran it was Churchill who suggested that the Curzon
Line be accepted as Poland's post-war eastern frontier.  The
Soviet claim to this boundary had been stated as early as
December, 1941, during Eden's visit to Moscow, but Churchill was
unwilling at that stage to make any territorial concessions
affecting Poland.  By the time of the Tehran Conference the
Curzon Line had become for the Soviets the starting point for
negotiations on the Polish-Soviet border.  Not even the pro-
Russian Union of the Polish Patriots could move Stalin on
this.(21)  He consistently pointed out that the Curzon Line had
been proposed, after all, by people who were no friends of
Bolshevik Russia.  The Curzon proposal, in 1920, had been
advanced without Russia's side having even been listened to,
while the Polish case had been fully heard and considered.
"Now," said Stalin, "some people want us to be less Russian than
Curzon or Clemenceau."

Meantime, the emigre government in London insisted on the
principle that Poland's pre-war eastern frontier was inviolable,
magnifying in this way the territorial issue so that it touched
on the question of Poland's future political system, if not its
independence.

Prime Minister Churchill explained that:  "If the Polish
government had taken the advice we tendered them . . . the
additional complication produced by the formation of the Polish
National Committee of Liberation at Lublin would not have
arisen, and anything like a prolonged delay in the settlement
can only have the effect of increasing the division between
Poles in Poland and also of hampering the common action which
the Poles, the Russians and the rest of the Allies are taking
against Germany."(22)

Moscow was left with practically no alternative but to
confront the London Poles with a policy of faits accomplis.  A
new opportunity came when the Red Army on July 22, 1944, crossed
the Bug River, which corresponded to the Curzon Line, and
captured Chelm, the first town of any size in the area.  Immediately, members of the Union of Polish Patriots created the
Polish Committee of National Liberation which issued the so-
called "Chelm Manifesto."

The manifesto appealed to Poles to fight the Germans for
the liberation of Poland and for a return of Pomerania, Oppeln,
Silesia, East Prussia and broad access to the Baltic.  While it
made vast claims to German territories, it was vague on the
precise definition of Poland's future Western frontiers.  It
also stated that the only possible protection against the
"pressure of German imperialism" was the construction of a
"great Slavic dam" based on Polish-Soviet-Czechoslovak cooperation.  It implied that the recognition of the Curzon Line as
the Polish-Soviet border was a precondition to any mutual
understanding among all Slavic nations that Polish territories

should belong to Poland, and that Ukrainian, White Russian and Lithuanian territories should belong to the Ukrainian, Byelo-russian and Lithuanian Soviet Socialist Republics.

On July 27, the Polish Committee of National Liberation, claiming to be the legitimate representative of the Polish nation, signed a treaty in Moscow with the Soviet Union recognizing the Curzon Line as the Soviet-Polish frontier. For the Polish leftists, any territorial concessions involved in accepting the Curzon Line were greatly overbalanced by the territorial, social and economic advantages gained from Moscow's pledge to secure the Oder-Neisse line, including the city of Szczecin (Stettin), as Poland's border with Germany.(23) It was pointed out that in the East, the Poles were always the "nation of masters," while all others were workers and peasants. In the West, as they saw it, the situation was just the reverse: The Poles were workers and peasants subjugated by Prussian junkers and bourgeois. The logical conclusion was that the westward movement of the Polish state would have the character of a social revolution in addition to liquidating an "arsenal of German imperialism."(24)

In any event, this was the only territorial configuration acceptable to the Russians, a reality that the Polish Socialists and the nationally oriented Communists understood. Once it was plain that Sikorski's proposal--of a Jagiellonian Poland enjoying friendly relations with the Soviet Union--would not satisfy Russian ambitions, they were the first to offer the best possible alternative--Piast Poland.

## The Oder-Neisse Line

Moscow was quick to make permanent its frontier with Poland. But it decided to leave to the Peace Conference final settlement of the new Polish-German border.

With the establishment of a pro-Soviet regime in Poland and the implications of that for Poland's post-war orientation, an unexpected development took place--the British and Americans became antithetical to Poland's territorial interests in the West. As the end of the war drew near, the Western allies came to realize that the ultimate solution of the Polish territorial question would have a direct bearing on what was going to happen with Germany, whose political fate--a vital issue--was still undecided.

The German and Polish issues had become closely inter-related. With Poland already lost, the Western powers began to look upon the future Germany as a form of protection against the Soviet danger. Churchill, an early proponent of compensating Poland in the West for territorial concessions in the East, began to take a considerable dislike to the concept. At one point, he said, "It would be a pity to stuff the Polish goose so full of German feed that he (would) die of indigestion."(25)

The final resolution of the Potsdam Conference (July 16-August 2, 1945) advised that:

> The final delimitation of the western frontier of Poland should await the peace settlement . . . Pending the final determination of Poland's western frontier, the former German territories east of a line running from the Baltic Sea immediately west of Swinemunde, and hence along the Oder river to the confluence of the Eastern Neisse River and along the western Neisse to the Czechoslovak frontier, including that portion of East Prussia not placed under the administration of the Union of Soviet Socialist Republics in accordance with the understanding reached at this conference and including the area of the former free city of Danzig, shall be under the administration of the Polish state and for such purposes should not be considered as part of the Soviet zone of occupation in Germany. (26)

Thus Poland was granted a right to "administer" the "former" German territories east of the Oder-Neisse line. This right had been combined with authority to arrange transfer of German population from Polish territory, (27) which, in Warsaw's view applied first of all to the Oder-Neisse land. The Peace Conference concluding World War II was to finalize this process. The initial understanding of this part of the Potsdam Protocol was that it was intended to delay the acceptance of an already accomplished fact.(28) But its vague construction opened the door for flexible interpretation. Soon this provision became a very useful diplomatic weapon: By questioning the permanence of the Oder-Neisse line, the Western powers could try to compel

Warsaw to adopt a pro-Western attitude. Simultaneously, it
served to win the Germans to the Western side.

The provision had advantages for the Soviet Union as well.
By redrawing Poland's western frontier and turning approximately
one-fourth of Germany over to Poland, Moscow aimed not only at
improving its own strategic position in Europe, but also at
magnifying the Polish-German conflict to an extent that would
prevent forever any genuine reconciliation. The imperfect legal
aspect of the territorial provision prolonged Polish dependence
on the Soviet Union and placed the Poles at odds with their
other wartime allies. In addition, it served as a safeguard
against Polish assertiveness which might lead to an attempt to
escape from Russian tutelage. Should Poland attempt to assert
its independence or should the Communist Party prove unable to
establish itself as a ruling elite, the Red Army was always
ready to act on behalf of Poland's security vis-a-vis Germany.

In consequence, from the moment of the Potsdam Agreement,
the paramount goal of Polish foreign policy was to secure
recognition of the Oder-Neisse line as the permanent Polish-
German border. Warsaw made its purpose clear, informing the
West of its view of the potential consequences which would
result from any attempt to change the border. When the Polish
foreign minister, W. Rzymowski, signed the United Nations
Charter on October 16, 1945, he pointed out that the conditions
of peace in Europe depended on the "inviolability of Polish
frontiers".(29) In effect, the Polish minister assumed that the
European peace was contingent on Allied policies in Germany
recognizing the finality of the Oder-Neisse Line. Thus, according to the Poles, it was the specific responsibility of the Big
Three to prevent revanchism in Germany.

In order to convey to the Western powers the importance to
Poland of their recognition of the new western border, Poland's
ambassador to the United States, Oscar Lange went so far as to
say that "if . . . Great Britain would support the Oder line . . .
and Russia opposed, you would find Poland voting with Britain." (30)
The implication was that the new regime in Poland valued national
interest above its alliance with the Soviet Union.

Initial reaction in the West to the part of the Potsdam
Agreement regarding Poland's border with Germany was well
expressed by President Truman. Reporting on the conference,
Truman said the agreement was a "compromise solution . . .
necessary . . . to enable the new Poland to organize itself and
to permit the speedier withdrawal of the armed forces which had
liberated her from the Germans." He continued by saying that
"the territory the Poles are to administer will enable Poland
better to support its population. It will provide a short and
more easily defensible frontier between Poland and Germany."

Poland was to "administer" these territories, but neither
Truman nor the Potsdam protocol indicated that the administration was temporary. One could assume that the "administration" was to be permanent, particularly since it involved the
right to expel all Germans still living in the region,
resettling the area with Poles from former eastern Poland. Such

rearrangement, in Truman's words, would "provide a more homo-
genous (Polish) nation." This was also the conclusion of the
New York Times, which, referring to Truman's report, observed:
"It is apparent . . . that the decision formulated at Potsdam
represents a definite settlement."(31)

Still, the Warsaw regime wanted an airtight claim to
present at the Peace Conference. Expecting the conference to
take place within two years of Potsdam, the Polish authorities
had to have the process of population resettlement completed
before the issue of the western border was to be discussed
again.

So, instead of preparing for a democratic election "as soon
as possible," the provisional government preferred to establish
itself as speedily "as possible on the western Neisse, the Oder
and the Baltic."(32) The ensuing Polish expulsion of the
Germans violated the Potsdam requirement that the transfer of
Germans "be effected in an orderly and humane manner."(33)
Although the Western powers consented to an agreement of the
Allied Control Council concerning the transfer to Germany of the
German population of Poland and other neighboring countries,
Polish excesses against the German population still remaining in
the Oder-Neisse territories led to additional serious doubts
about the wisdom of the Potsdam Agreement.

More than a month before the Big Three met in Potsdam, the
provisional government in Warsaw issued a decree of "Expulsion
of Hostile Elements from Polish Society."(34) It was a unilateral act of incorporation which authorized the forced expulsion
of the Germans. Since time was of critical importance to the
Poles, the Germans were often given only two hours evacuation
notice and were allowed to take with them no more than about
forty pounds of personal belongings; there were some cases where
notice of no more than ten minutes was given. Because of the
lack of the medical care, food, accommodations and fuel, the
incidence of sickness and death among the deported Germans was
very high. Persons with Polish surnames were required to accept
Polish citizenship because they were regarded as having been
forcibly Germanized. The Polish regime wanted to demonstrate
that its claim to the Oder-Neisse territories was not purely
strategic. Strategic or not, the expulsion of the Germans was
chaotic and painful, causing concern among even the Russians,
who made attempts to halt it for a while.(35)

The Western powers were gravely concerned over the expulsions. They feared that the sudden influx of millions of
additional people would cause widespread hunger in the Western
occupation zones of Germany.

Lacking any effective international sanctions against
Warsaw, Great Britain argued that the Poles should not expect
the West to honor the terms of the Potsdam Protocol which were
favorable to Poland while the Poles were shirking their responsi
bilities under the agreement. Foreign Secretary Bevin asked for
Soviet, French and American help to "stop this ghastly process,"
and declared in the House of Commons that the British government
was not committed to support the Oder-Neisse line. Thus, Polish

treatment of the Germans was to become critical in resolving the question of frontiers.

At the same time, the Polish-Soviet interpretation of another provision of the Potsdam Protocol alarmed the Western powers. Describing the course of the Polish-German border, the protocol stated that it should be "a line running from the Baltic Sea immediately west of Swinemunde and thence along the Oder River." A change in the wording of this provision took place at the last moment, at Stalin's suggestion. According to Truman, the first version read that the border should be a "line running from the Baltic Sea through Swinemunde," but Stalin proposed "west of," to replace "through." How far west? asked Truman. "Immediately west of," was Stalin's reply, and such wording was approved.(36)

Without even mentioning the big inland port of Stettin (Szczecin), most of which is on the west bank of the Oder, the Soviets were seeking a way to turn it over to Poland. The Soviet interpretation was that the border should be drawn west of Swinemunde straight south to the point where the line crossed the Oder, and then "along" the Oder--instead of from Swinemunde directly to the mouth of the river. Thus, the Poles were to "administer" the entire city of Stettin, together with several hundred square kilometers of territory on the west bank of the river. In this way, Stalin kept his agreement with the Polish Committee of National Liberation to turn the city over to Poland.(37)

But the Soviet action was not taken without some hesitation. The so-called "marriage of Poland with the sea" took place in Kolobrzeg (Kolberg), not in Stettin, and three times at least the Poles had taken over administration of the city.(38) Polish authority was not fully established until March, 1946, when the city and the entire industrial district were completely looted by the Russians.(39)

For the West, this was another example of joint Polish-Soviet violation of Potsdam. Poland was accused of expelling the Germans under conditions that conflicted with the orderly manner prescribed by the Big Three, and of annexing additional territory in advance of the Peace Conference.

Since London and Washington had little effective influence on the Communists in Poland, the Western allies decided once again to use the leverage of the finality of the Oder-Neisse line.

Secretary Bevin stated that he had "never . . . been able to reconcile (the new Polish western frontier) with the Atlantic Charter."(40) His statement was followed by one from the Germans, who by that time--it was 1946--were regaining political self-confidence, and suggested a revision of Germany's eastern border.(41) The worst was yet to come.

Speaking in Stuttgart on September 6, 1946, Secretary of State James Byrnes declared that the U.S. government was not committed to the Oder-Neisse line. Brynes noted that Poland had been forced to yield its eastern territories to the Soviet Union in exchange for revision of its western borders. But, he said, "the extent of this area to be ceded to Poland" was to await future determination. Byrnes explained that "with respect to Silesia and other eastern German areas, the assignments to Poland by Russia for administrative purposes took place before the Potsdam meeting . . . (and) the heads of governments did not agree to support at the Peace Conference the cession of this particular area." Finally, he narrowly defined the purpose of Polish administration, avoiding comment about the right of the Poles to expel the German population. In his opinion, the Polish task was to "reorganize the economic life in these areas."(42)

Thus did the United States make a choice between Germany and Poland, between Adenauer and Mikolajczyk. Elections in Germany were forthcoming. The United States wanted to win the Germans over to the Western side and nothing could be more appealing to the Germans than territorial and national unity.

Nor was Moscow far behind in a willingness to sacrifice Poland. The Soviets secretly indicated they were eager to revise the western Polish frontier and return Silesia to Germany in exchange for unquestionable Soviet dominion over Poland. In a subsequent proposal, the Soviet Union included a demand for Western non-interference in all of Eastern Europe. The United states refused.(43)

The possibility of a new Polish partition--inherent in the German issue--forced Warsaw to adopt a policy that mirrored Adenauer's. Adenauer calculated that by making the Federal Republic America's most faithful ally in Western Europe he would win territory and national unity for the Germans should the "roll-back" doctrine succeed. Warsaw, on the other hand, desired to stay wedded to the Russians, counting on them to preserve the status quo in Europe. Unable to solve their mutual problems directly, the Poles and West Germans sought maximum integration into their respective block for the achievement of direct access to the chief contestants, hoping thereby that the eventual success of their guardians would be their own. The traditional Polish-German duel was elevated from the regional level to become one of the chief issues of the global Cold War.

The Poles got what they wanted from Moscow, but not until the Soviet leadership learned that its feeler to the Germans had failed. When the Communists lost elections in all Western zones of Germany (and in response to Brynes' Stuttgart speech), Molotov acknowledged that the Potsdam Conference had left the Polish-German frontier to be defined by the peace treaty with Germany. But he made his purpose clear by saying that that was merely a "formal point of view," since "whoever would have dreamt of the transfer of Germans as undertaken merely for the sake of a short-term experiment?" Then, some four weeks later, the Polish premier received personal assurances from Stalin, allowing him to state triumphantly that "Generalissimo Stalin told us that those who wish to shake our western frontiers, which were set at Potsdam, would not only have to deal with the Polish Army but also with the Red Army."(44)

The German Communists were charged with the task of winning the Germans over to the Soviet side, but they were doing poorly. Only in the Russian occupation zone, where voting results could

be manufactured, was the Communist Party able to "win" a majority. Having in fact very few admissable excuses for failure
(neither ideology nor the Russians could be blamed), the Communists had to point to the popular resentment aroused by the
cession of eastern German lands to Poland. There is no doubt
that even a minor revision would have improved their ability to
appeal to the German nation. Unlike other Communist parties in
Eastern Europe, which had always had nationalism as a weapon in
reserve, the German Communists were left only with ideology.

It is not surprising that Walter Ulbricht, deputy chairman
of the East German Socialist Unity (Communist) Party, was
unhappy with the existing territorial arrangements and he made
no secret of his views. The Oder-Neisse line, according to
Ulbricht, was a British idea which had only been accepted by the
Soviet Union "as a faithful ally," but it served the wrong
purpose; Great Britain had desired to strengthen the Polish
"reactionary" emigrees. He continued by saying that the decision had not been final, and that when the war ended, it had
been within the Soviet power to alter this political mistake.
The "Soviet Union awaited developments in Germany, [and] a
democratic Germany could have influenced the completion of this
territorial transfer [while] the reactionary . . . parties in
West Germany made it impossible."(45)

Having failed to expand their influence over the Western
zones of occupation, the East German Communists had to abandon
hope for any territorial revisions. After the decision was made
to create the East German state, Poland was able to secure a
promise that one of East Germany's first international acts
would be to sign in July 1950 a treaty with Poland recognizing
the Oder-Neisse line as the permanent frontier.

Implicitly claiming authority to act in the name of the
entire German nation, the government of the German Democratic
Republic agreed in Zgorzelec (Gorlitz) with another puppet--the
government of the Polish People's Republic--that the "established and existing frontier . . . constitutes the state frontier between Poland and Germany."(46) This wording later became
known as the "Zgorzelec Formula," and was flexible enough for
both German states and Poland to support this form of
recognition. The border question had been settled conclusively
between Poland and a German state, while preserving the power of
the Big Four (the Soviet Union included) and the future united
Germany to make the "final" decision on this issue during the
Peace Conference with Germany. "The Zgorzelec Formula," therefore, did not involve full recognition, and its obvious
advantage was that it did not violate the rights of the Big Four
which had been established by the Potsdam Agreement.

It is worthwhile noting that unlike all the other treaties
between Communist Poland and the rest of the Soviet bloc, the
Zgorzelec Agreement had a very limited purpose. It was not a
treaty of "friendship and mutual assistance," the standard form
used by Moscow for arranging relations between "socialist"
states. The Polish-East German Treaty was decidedly without
effusiveness and flamboyant courtesies and no mutual obligation
was imposed to protect the signatories against any aggression.

Nor were there any special provisions for "fraternal" relations. The treaty was designed to serve one specific purpose--the delineation of the Polish-German frontier.

The Polish military buildup on the Western border and Warsaw's insistence on maintaining the Red Army in East Germany following Polish recognition of the German Democratic Republic are the best evidence of just how strained relations were between these two Communist regimes.

Despite its legal and political deficiencies, the Zgorzelec Agreement should be regarded as a major victory for the Polish Communists. From the moment the Soviets granted Poland the administration of the Oder-Neisse territories, the Polish right to control this area was questioned, not only by the Western powers, but sometimes by the Soviets themselves. As we have seen the East Germans were to make the argument that minor revisions in the frontier would advance the cause of communism in Germany. If Moscow had agreed to such changes it would have constituted a most unfortunate precedent. That no revision took place was primarily due to the fact that the Russians could not extract the price they wanted from the West, namely, recognition of Eastern Europe as the Soviet sphere of influence. Thus not until five years after the end of the war was the finality of the Oder-Neisse line acknowledged, even within the Soviet bloc, by an international agreement. The Soviet-Polish Treaty of April 21, 1945, for example, did not even mention Poland's western border, and the Soviet Union had no formal obligation to protect its integrity.

The Polish-East German Treaty was the direct cause of a diplomatic and propaganda war between Poland and West Germany. Even before East Germany recognized the Oder-Neisse line, the government of the Federal Republic proclaimed its determination to recover lost German territories. In his first official declaration in the Bundestag, Chancellor Adenauer, who was also foreign minister, called the Oder-Neisse line "illegal," since, he said, it violated the Atlantic Charter of 1941, the Potsdam Agreement and the rights of the German nation. On the same occasion, the leader of the Socialist opposition, Dr. Kurt Schumacher, warned against any compromise and advocated forma- tion of a "strong base for a political struggle against the Oder-Neisse line."(47) Both major parties in West Germany endorsed a foreign policy aimed at revising the territorial status quo.

When East Germany declared its support of the new border and concluded a formal treaty with Poland, Adenauer enumerated conditions for the solution of the Polish-German dispute. First, the Peace Conference was to be the only place where the territorial question could be discussed; second, before such a conference could take place, the unification of Germany had to be arranged, with the West German government recognized as the sole steward of the German nation; third, Poland and the Soviet Union had to recognize the Oder-Neisse territories as being under only temporary Polish administration; and finally, the regime in Poland had to become "democratic."(48)

Not surprisingly, the West German conditions were regarded
in the East as an attempt to reverse some of the major consequences of the Second World War, and West Germany was proclaimed
to be a country of "war criminals," "fascists," "racists,"
"militarists," "revanchists," etc., who survived only as a
result of the support of "American bayonets" and American
capital.(49)

The first opportunity for a direct Polish-West German
settlement of the border issue was created by political changes
in Poland brought about by the return to power of a "national"
Communist leadership.

In December, 1956, the West German foreign minister,
Heinrich von Brentano, visited Poland. The purpose of his visit
was to find out for the Christian Democratic government whether
Poland would agree to some sort of compromise on the border
question. This was unacceptable to the Poles and von Brentano's
mission failed. But days later, when Helmut Kalbizer, a Social
Democratic member of the Bundestag, arrived in Warsaw on a
visit, he was informed that the Poles were very much interested
in reconciliation with the West Germans, and would welcome
diplomatic relations and trade without formal recognition of the
Oder-Neisse frontier.(50)

Polish motives were plain. Exchange of diplomatic envoys
would imply de facto recognition of the Oder-Neisse border and
would facilitate the West German government's presentation of
this fact to its people. At the same time, Poland would gain
some form of recognition, access to West German markets and the
opportunity to obtain financial credits for the purchase of
German products.

But the ruling Christian Democratic Party had not been
prepared to grant even implied respect for the Oder-Neisse line.
Territorial revision and unification had so strong an appeal
among the West Germans that any modification of this political
program was thought to be too costly.

It meant, in practice, that politicians in West Germany
could not risk telling their people that the international
realities were so adverse to the goal of unification that there
was no chance for it in the foreseeable future. Chancellor
Adenauer was asked to comment on this fact. The question was
whether "any politician in Germany (would) survive politically
if he said he had given up hope of recovering the territories
beyond the Oder-Neisse line." He left this issue unanswered and
continued to insist that Poland must first recognize the right
of the expelled to their homeland, and that reconciliation would
have to be preceded by "the integration (of these territories)
into a superior economic system, such as the Coal and Steel
Community, or the Common Market, and then . . . it would be
quite easy to find a solution also to (the) political questions."(51)

In fact, very little had changed in Adenauer's policy
toward Poland. He no longer questioned the legitimacy of the
Polish regime, but he continued to insist on territorial revisions. As a consequence, Gomulka's first bid to West Germany
failed.

New hope appeared in Warsaw when President de Gaulle
declared that all of Germany's post-war borders must be accepted
as permanent before German unification could be possible.  He
said:

> The reunion of the two parts into a single Germany
> which would be entirely free seems to us the normal
> destiny of the German people, provided they do not
> call into question their present frontiers in the
> west, the east, the north and the south, and that they
> move themselves one day in a contractual organization
> of all Europe for cooperation, liberty and peace. (52)

After France recognized the Oder-Neisse line, the Poles
approached the United States for a similar statement.  According
to the Potsdam Agreement, all matters relating to territorial
changes were reserved for the authority of the great powers;
thus, American recognition of Oder-Neisse would be valued above
any declaration on the part of West Germany.
     Once again the Poles failed.  In reply to the Polish note,
the United States said that a decision in this regard must await
the Peace Conference with the "entire German people."(53)
Implicitly, the American government endorsed the West German
claim for unification and recognition of the right to a homeland
before final settlement of the Polish-German border could be
achieved.
     For the Polish government this was direct evidence that the
Western bloc had decided to adopt a multilateral approach to the
issue of the Oder-Neisse frontier.  Once again the Poles were
left with no alternative but to further their integration within
the Soviet bloc.  Consequently, in the beginning of 1961, when
the Federal Republic expressed a willingness to sign a non-
aggression treaty with Poland, Warsaw refused, since such a
treaty would create an opportunity for Bonn to "swallow" East
Germany.(54)  Finally, the regimes of Poland and East Germany
were brought close together and began to develop a united front
against the Federal Republic.
     Meantime, developments were taking place in West Germany
and Poland that would prove embarrassing to each of the regimes.
     Figures showed that a growing number of West Germans,
including those expelled from the eastern territories, were no
longer interested in returning east of the Oder-Neisse and that
an increasing number of Germans considered these territories
lost forever:  in 1953, 11 percent; in 1964, 46 percent; in
1968, 56 percent.  At the same time, the number of respondents
who were opposed to recognition of the Oder-Neisse frontier
dropped from 80 percent in 1951, to 59 percent in 1964, to 33
percent in 1967.(55)
     The government in Bonn continued to restate its old policy
in spite of declining political support for it.  The majority of
those who had been expelled were already assimilated by West
German society.  As early as 1955 some officials had felt that
the process of integration should be confined to the economic
and political realms, while cultural integration should be

slowed down, if not prevented, since it could weaken German claims to the territories east of the Oder and Neisse Rivers.(56)

Influential church groups in West Germany and Poland entered the debate. The West German Evangelical Church circulated a memorandum advocating reconciliation instead of territorial restitution. For the time being, the memorandum urged, the legal issue should be put aside as less important than humanitarian considerations. The Roman Catholic Church was first to take a similar initiative on behalf of Poland. In preparation for celebration of the Polish national and religious millennium, the Polish Episcopate addressed to the German bishops a letter which attempted to explain Poland's insistence on the Oder-Neisse line. "We grant forgiveness," said the Polish bishops, "and we ask your forgiveness." In their reply, the German bishops employed the same phrase.(57)

The regime in Warsaw was furious. Here was the church daring to speak in the name of the Polish nation at the same time the Communist Party was conducting a campaign aimed at discrediting the church. The authorities accused the church of playing politics and they attributed to the Polish bishops the belief that Nazi crimes in Poland had been offset by the way in which the Communist authorities had expelled German residents from the Oder-Neisse territories right after the war.

Chancellor Ludwig Erhard, Adenauer's successor, published a "peace note" indicating that his government intended to adopt a more accommodating approach to the German problem and the issue of European security. From the Polish perspective, however, Erhard's proposals were unacceptable since Erhard left intact the Bonn formula which demanded German reunification first, then free elections, an all-German government and then a peace conference where the territorial questions could be considered. "According to international law, Germany still exists within the borders of December 31, 1937," Erhard declared.(58)

Hans-Georg Kiesinger, who followed Erhard, was the first West German chancellor to introduce a fresh approach. In his inaugural address in the Bundestag (December 13, 1966), he proclaimed a willingness to respect the Oder-Neisse frontier until the Peace Conference with a united Germany could determine the final state of affairs.

Polish Premier Jozef Cyrankiewicz replied the Kiesinger version of Ostpolitik had the same purpose as the foreign policies of the previous Bonn governments, that is, to "reverse the effects of the German defeat." The Polish premier again accused Bonn of seeking territorial revision in a policy directed against the peace and security of Europe. It had been a change of tone and tactics on Bonn's part, but not of its foreign policy objectives.(59)

Polish reserve was based on the fact that the German demarche was combined with the insistence on German reunification within the 1937 borders. Warsaw's acceptance of this new German proposal could have been interpreted as an endorsement of the German legal claim to the Oder-Neisse territories. Another source of Polish reluctance to negotiate was that Poland wanted

Bonn to abandon its aim of reunification under West German
auspices.  Poland had already adopted a multilateral approach
and viewed the new Ostpolitik as no more than "a propaganda
maneuver . . . intended to isolate the GDR."(60)

The path to direct Polish-West German negotiations was
finally cleared with the arrival in power of Willy Brandt's
Social Democrats in coalition with the liberal Free Democrats.
Brandt was now in a position to carry out his conciliatory
policy toward Germany's Slavic neighbors, especially Poland.
The immediate formal obstacles were removed when the West German
government signed the Nuclear Non-Proliferation Treaty (NPT).
This was an important change in Germany's foreign policy.  (For
Adenauer, the treaty had been a "squared Morgenthau plan," and
Franz-Josef Strauss had described it as "Versailles in cosmic
size."(61)  Russia and Poland reciprocated by dropping their
demand that Bonn recognize the East German regime as a precondition for reconciliation.

Directly challenging Adenauer's belief that Europe did not
extend beyond the Elbe,(62) Brandt declared:

Europe ends neither on the Elbe nor on the Polish
eastern frontier.  Russia is indissolubly bound up in
the history of Europe, not only as an opponent and a
peril, but also as a partner--historically, politically culturally and economically.  Only when we in
Western Europe fasten our attention on this partnership, only when the nations of Eastern Europe realize
this, too, can we come to a balancing of interests. (63)

It was logical for Brandt to conclude, therefore, that
normalization of Polish-German relations would have the same
historical importance as the friendship between Germany and
France."(64)

The significance of Brandt's foreign policy was in the
rearrangement of priorities.  Brandt proposed to reverse the
traditional order of unification, elections and territorial
negotiations, and to begin with recognition of the political and
territorial status quo as a first step toward the ultimate goal,
reunification.

Following Brandt's electoral victory and his resulting
break with West German foreign policy, Gomulka faced a choice of
whether to support Ulbricht's demand that Bonn's formal recognition of East Germany precede East European talks with West
Germany or to ignore Ulbricht and negotiate directly with Bonn.
In the event, the decision was made by the Soviets who began
making their own arrangements with the Federal Republic.  In
principle, Gomulka probably could have backed East Germany, on
practice, however, things were changing too rapidly for Poland
to drag its feet.

Gomulka ordered an end to anti-German rhetoric and in 1969
cast a favorable eye on the new Ostpolitik:  "One cannot fail to
appreciate the fact," Gomulka said, "that from the political
point of view, the SPD formula on the recognition by the Federal

Republic of the frontier on the Oder and Neisse constitutes a
step forward in comparison to the stand taken on this issue by
all the previous Federal Republic governments." He proposed
talks on the normalization of relations.(65) Brandt agreed (66)
and soon representatives of both countries met for the first
time since the infamous Polish-German non-aggression pact was
concluded in 1934.

Polish-German negotiations could hardly have been easy,
preceded as they were by a thousand years of antagonism, culmin-
ating most recently with the Nazi crimes in Poland and then with
Polish expulsion of the Germans after the war.

Several issues required clarification, but only two were of
special importance: first, the agreement concerning territorial
integrity and the recognition of the Polish-German border; and
second, the fate of the ethnic Germans still living in Poland.

The Oder-Neisse issue was surely the most crucial, and
regardless of all the propaganda, the Zgorzelec Agreement and
repeated Soviet assurances, the Poles were quite aware that the
Oder-Neisse line was not legally a permanent international
frontier. They insisted, therefore, that the negotiated treaty
include a clause acknowledging the new border as the "final"
international boundary between Poland and Germany.

The initial draft of the treaty contained the words "final"
and "recognition," (67) but the West Germans opposed that
formulation for two reasons.

First, the Federal Republic unilaterally could not make a
decisive statement in that regard, since, according to the
Potsdam Agreement, the right to "final" settlement of the
territorial question was explicitly reserved by the Great Powers
themselves, and could be implemented only at the all-German
Peace Conference. According to the West German spokesman:

> The rights and responsibilities of the four powers
> for Berlin and for Germany as a whole continue to
> exist and our treaty agreements with the Western
> powers must not be affected . . . Bilateral agreements
> between the Federal Republic and Poland cannot replace
> a peace settlement for Germany as a whole. (68)

The second consideration was that Brandt's coalition would
not be able to secure ratification of a treaty that contained
"final recognition" of the Oder-Neisse line because such ratification would entail a constitutional amendment requiring a two-
thirds majority. This was because the Basic Law (Constitution)
of the Federal Republic declared that Germany existed within its
1937 borders. For a workable solution the Poles would have to
compromise.

Since Warsaw was unable to obtain "final recognition" of
the border, it insisted on the strongest possible wording in its
stead. The treaty stated that:

> The existing boundary line whose course is laid down
> in Chapter IX of the Decisions of the Potsdam Confer-
> ence of 2 August 1945 . . . shall constitute the

western state frontier of the People's Republic of
Poland.
They (the Federal Republic and Poland) reaffirm the
inviolability of the existing frontiers now and in the
future . . . .
They declare that they have no territorial claims
whatsoever against each other and that they will not
assert such claims in the future. (69)

In the strict sense of international law, the Federal
Republic recognized the Oder-Neisse line only as a de facto
border. The treaty said nothing more than that the border
followed the line agreed on at Potsdam. As Whetten explains,
West Germany

. . . had not ceded to the Polish government its
legal claims to the Eastern territories, though it
renounced the desire for their restitution. The
normalization treaty was subordinated to the Potsdam
and Paris Agreements thereby upholding the Allies,
reservations about the final disposition of the
respective territorial claims. (70)

In order to stress this point and leave no doubt about the
precise significance the Federal Republic attached to this
wording, the Bonn government sent separate notes to the United
States, Great Britain and France, assuring them that the treaty
was not intended to infringe on their rights as victors in the
Second World War.
From a constitutional standpoint, the treaty upheld the
West German claim that Germany existed within its 1937 borders.
The treaty did not contradict Chancellor Erhard's statement of
1966 that this legal fiction could be changed only when a freely
elected all-German government decided to do so. This claim was
endorsed by the Legal Committee of the West German Bundesrat,
which declared that the treaty did not violate the Basic Law.
In particular, the committee endorsed Article 79, which provided
that "with respect to international treaties whose subject is a
peace settlement . . . it is required to obtain . . . the
affirmative vote of two-thirds of the members of the Bundestag
and two-thirds of the members of the Bundesrat."(71)
Actually, both sides accepted the Zgorzelec formula, which
included neither the word "final" nor the term "recognition."
The treaty was an official acknowledgement of the existing
political reality and a renunciation of territorial claims and
the use of force. But it was not a document resolving the
problems in a legal sense. The greatest advantage for Poland in
all this was the reference to Potsdam, vindicating the Polish
interpretation of the Agreement. That is, the original intention of the big powers was to make the Oder-Neisse line the
permanent Polish-German border, and only the legal side of the
grant needed confirmation at the Peace Conference. "Final
recognition" of the frontier would still await a peace conference and the Basic Law still required either a constitutional

amendment repealing the concept of "Germany with the frontiers
of December 31, 1937," or another treaty between a united
Germany and Poland. The Federal Republic claimed to have no
authority to relinquish territories in the name of Germany (72)
a claim of somewhat dubious merit since Bonn continued to assert
the right to sole representation of Germany.

Poland decided to read the treaty as an agreement consti-
tuting recognition: "This historical act, added to the Treaty
with the GDR concluded in Zgorzelec back in 1950, form(s) a
legal and political recognition of the final nature of the
Polish frontier on the Oder and Neisse."(73) By this the Poles
did not intend to challenge the letter of the Potsdam Agreement,
just the West German premise that the Germany of 1937 still
existed legally. For Warsaw the political reality was that
there were two German states and that each of them had made a
separate treaty with Poland regarding recognition of Poland's
western boundary. Thus as far as Poland was concerned, the
problem was settled. This Polish interpretation implicitly
disregarded the West German pretense that only Bonn had the
right to represent Germany.

The Treaty, said Polish Foreign Minister Jedrychowski,
"settled difficult issues that derive from an exceedingly
difficult past."(74) There is no question that the Polish-
German relations had been tragic, and during the negotiations
the Poles strove to have it put on record that they had been on
the "good" side, at least in the case of the Second World War.
The Poles requested that the preamble of the treaty state that
the Germans bore moral responsibility--in fact, guilt--for the
war. Such a statement would have given psychological comfort to
the Poles and would have provided justification for the
uncompromising attitude of the Polish regime which had been
producing intensely anti-German propaganda during the preceding
twenty-five years.

Not surprisingly, such an admission of guilt was unacceptable. Still, the Poles insisted on some reference to the war,
that:

> More than twenty-five years have passed since the end
> of the Second World War of which Poland became the
> first victim and which inflicted great suffering on
> the nations of Europe.

The Poles explained the importance to them of even that
slender reference:

> In these words we have a terse allusion to history, a
> simple reference to the past . . . . That said, it is
> still a fact that never before in the thousand year
> history of her statehood, not even during the parti-
> tions, has Poland endured anything even remotely
> comparable with the horrors inflicted by German
> fascism during the Second World War: six million
> people--twenty-two percent of our population--lost
> their lives. (75)

Next, the treaty pointed in a general way to the necessity of improving international relations in Europe, declaring that disputes should be settled by peaceful means. Poland and West Germany pledged to "refrain from any threat or use of force in matters affecting European and international security and in their mutual relations."

This provision of the treaty prohibits both parties from using force not only in their mutual relations, but also in their relations with other states in Europe. Potentially, this treaty therefore could provide Polish government with a pretext for declining to participate in the police actions of the Warsaw Pact, such as that of Czechoslovakia in 1968. One must recognize, however, that a quite different interpretation can be applied to this obligation (the invasion of Czechoslovakia had not been described by the participants as a military action, but as an act of "fraternal help"). But Warsaw must bear in mind that its violation of the treaty would provide West Germany with the best excuse possible to do the same, and in the case of bilateral relations, the Federal Republic is clearly the stronger party. The most logical reason for the inclusion of the clause seems to be that the Poles do not wish to act as a gendarme in Eastern Europe. Inclusion of the provision seems to have been deliberate; the Soviet-West German treaty contains no such prohibition.

Finally, the treaty calls for full normalization of relations, for a "broadening of . . . cooperation in the sphere of economic, scientific, technological, cultural and other relations . . . in their mutual interest." An important component of Brandt's Ostpolitik was a reliance on economics. A strong and technologically advanced West Germany had a great deal to offer the Polish economy, which, despite enormous efforts and a considerable amount of progress, was still a generation behind industrial development in Western Europe. Warsaw was anxious to obtain credits, technological know-how and access to West German markets where agricultural products and some manufactured (whose main attraction was price) could provide Poland with badly needed hard currency. For its part, the Federal Republic was trying to expand its markets and gain additional sources of raw materials close at hand.

If guarantees of territorial integrity were paramount to the Poles in these negotiations, no less were the West Germans interested in resolving the question of ethnic Germans still living in Poland. It was one of the chief motives for Bonn's having sought a modus vivendi with Warsaw. Here the Poles had their way. They argued that it was strictly an internal matter. As a result there was no formal recognition of the problem in the treaty, but the West German government did manage to secure from the Polish government a unilateral declaration, called Information, which contained a promise to allow "any persons . . . owing to their indisputable ethnic German origin to leave to East or West Germany."(76) The document stated further that consideration would be given to the petitions of "mixed and separated families as well as . . . Polish nationals who, either because of their changed family situation or because of their earlier decision, express the wish to be reunited with near relatives." At the same time, a specific limitation was included, since the Polish government emphasized that no authorization to leave would be granted in the case of emigration motivated by higher wages ("for employment purposes," as the Information expressed it).

The German representatives were left with no guarantees that Poland would carry out its obligations under the Information. The West German foreign minister, in an attempt to exert what leverage Germany had, indicated that German ratification of the treaty would be greatly facilitated if Poland took rapid action on the repatriation issue.(77)

For the Germans this was a sensitive problem, both emotionally and constitutionally. Public opinion in West Germany was strongly influenced by the argument of philosopher Karl Jaspers that humanitarian considerations should always be given priority.(78) The legal side of the problem was that a number of persons living in Poland had dual Polish and German citizenship. Article 116 of the Basic Law defines a German citizen as follows:

> Unless otherwise provided by law, a German within the meaning of this Basic Law is a person who possesses German citizenship or who has been admitted to the territory of the German Reich as it existed on December 31, 1937, as a refugee or expellee of German stock or as the spouse or descendant of such person. (79)

Almost immediately, representatives delegated by the Red Cross from both countries met to negotiate a solution of technical matters and agreed that some 90,000 Germans would be granted permission to leave. Applications were to be directed to the Polish authorities alone and the decision in each case was to be determined by such factors as the language spoken at home, the nationality of the parents and the schools attended before 1945.

In mid-1971 the West German government proposed to renegotiate the issue, since it estimated that some 900,000 to 1,000,000 German nationals were still in Poland and that between 150,000 and 250,000 wished to emigrate. Warsaw, however, refused to discuss the question, raising doubts in Bonn about Polish sincerity and some dissatisfaction with the entire arrangement. As it was originally agreed, emigration began in December, 1970, at the rate of 2,000 to 3,000 persons a month.(80)

The final threshold over which the Oder-Neisse question had to pass before achieving status as a de facto international border was its ratification by the West German Bundestag. Again the proposed formula for ratification differed substantially from the Polish interpretation of the treaty, since the Federal Republic refused to consider the border as final. First of all, the agreement involves Poland and West Germany alone and in this case Bonn waived its claim to speak for all of Germany. In addition, it was not the "final" border in the meaning of Potsdam.

The treaty, therefore, had no effect on the West German assertion that the idea of a unified Germany was still alive as an ultimate goal of the German nation. In its territorial configuration, Germany was still that of December 31, 1937, while the present treaty was only an intermediary solution binding to the Federal Republic exclusively. The legal justification for any future claims to the Oder-Neisse territories made by Germany were not foreclosed.

However, before further territorial claims on Poland could be advanced, a fundamental re-examination of the German attitude toward Poland would have to take place. The moral dimension of Ostpolitik--reconciliation with Poland--was its central element and the treaty was viewed as a beginning of the process of reconciliation. This is a very special attribute of the Polish-West German treaty that was not emphasized as strongly in either the Soviet or Czechoslovakian treaties. Only in the case of Poland, Chancellor Brandt stated, was reconciliation made a "moral and political duty."(81)

The treaty was ratified, but with clear misgivings. One could not have expected the West Germans to be enthusiastic about abandoning what had been a primary emotional and political objective. For the Germans, it meant no less than consent to partition. Ratification became possible only because the great majority of Christian Democrats abstained. Only two hundred forty-eight delegates, out of the four hundred ninety-six members of the Bundestag cast affirmative votes, with seventeen voting against ratification. So only half the Bundestag supported the treaty.

Thus concluded a painful and bitter Polish-German dispute over the Oder-Neisse line. One must admit surprise that the controversy was resolved in so short a time and that as far as it is possible to predict, the Germans will refrain from questioning the finality of this border, barring a resurgence of nationalist extremism. The treaty is an undeniable achievement worthy of special emphasis, particularly given the Polish tradition of winning wars only to lose the peace.

Still, a correct evaluation of the Polish-West German treaty requires an understanding that the Soviet Union was very much an involved party. The treaty was an offspring of the much more important agreement regulating relations between Bonn and Moscow. In this case, Russia acted as Poland's patron, taking upon itself responsibility for safeguarding the territorial configuration of Europe, including the Oder-Neisse line. It had been Gomulka's plan to achieve normalization with West Germany independently of Moscow, but the actual agreement came as a consequence of the Soviet treaty. Basically, Bonn made peace with Russia, while Poland was a part of that larger relationship.

This does not mean that Poland emerged with no advantages. On the contrary, the Communists managed to convert the theory of "two enemies" into the practice of "two friends," and they must have felt less dependent on Soviet support as a result. The moral aspect of the treaty and the mutual desire for reconciliation--rather than official government declarations--might prove to be the most significant elements of the Polish-German dialogue. For this reason, the treaty has encouraged nationalism and political assertiveness on the part of the Poles, despite the fact that it was concluded under Soviet tutelage.

While the treaty provided a limited international success to the Warsaw regime, it was an unquestionable triumph at home for the views of the Roman Catholic Church whose representatives advanced the notion of Polish-German reconciliation long before the authorities had the courage to admit it was desirable and possible. Thus the church scored another victory over the party and the treaty proved to be little help to Gomulka. Only two weeks after the treaty was approved, Gomulka was forced to resign because of his negligent handling of the economy.

72

## Notes

1. Documents on Polish-Soviet Relations, 1939-1945, vol. I (London-Melbourne-Toronto:  Heinemann, General Sikorski Institute, 1961), p. 97.
Hereafter cited as DPSR.

2. DPSR, vol. I. p. 97.

3. DPSR, vol I, p. 128.

4. DPSR, vol. I, p. 129.

5. DPSR, vol. I, p. 129.

6. DPSR, vol. I, p. 142.

7. DPSR, vol. I, p. 144.

8. Edward J. Rozek, Wartime Diplomacy.  A Pattern in Poland (London:  John Wiley & Sons, Inc., 1958), p. 62.

9. DPSR, vol. I, pp. 117-8.

10. Rozek, op. cit., p. 59.

11. DPSR, vol. I, pp. 246-7.

12. DPSR, vol. I, pp. 244-5.

13. Rozek, op. cit., p. 94.

14. DPSR, vol. I, p. 457.

15. DPSR, vol. I, p. 265.

16. DPSR, vol. II, p. 72.

17. DPSR, vol II, p. 96.

18. Peter H. Stern, The Struggle for Poland (Washington, D.C.:  Public Affairs Press, 1953), p. 27.

19. Aleksander Bregman, Zakamarki Historii (Londyn:  Nakladem Polskiej Fundacji Kulturalnej, 1968), p. 182.

20. DPSR, vol. II, p. 98.

21. DPSR, vol. II, p. 770.

22. DPSR, vol. II, p. 444.

23. Polska Ludowa--Zwiazek Radziecki, 1944-1974.  Zbior Dokumentow i Materialow (Warszawa, 1974), p. 13.

24. Alfred Lampe, Miejsce Polski w Europie (Moskwa:  Nakladem Zwiazku Partiotow Polskich w ZSRR, 1944), p. 49.

25. Quoted in James F. Byrnes, Speaking Frankly (New York and London:  Harper Brothers Publishers, 1947).

26. Quoted in James T. Shotwell and Max M. Laserson, Poland and Russia 1919-1945 (New York:  King's Crown Press, 1945), pp. 110-11.

27. Gotthold Rhode and Wolfgang Wagner (eds), The Genesis of the Oder-Neisse Line (Stuttgart:  Brentano-Verlag, 1959), p. 257.

28. The New York Times, July 13, 1945.

29. Rzeczpospolita, October 18, 1945.

30. The New York Times, August 8, 1946.

31. The New York Times, August 10, 1945.

32. Premier Osobka-Morawski, quoted in The New York Times, July 22, 1945.

33. Rhode and Wagner, op. cit., p. 257.

34. Andrzej Lesniweski (ed.), Western Frontiers of Poland (Warsaw:  Polish Institute of International Affairs, 1965), pp. 83-4.

35. Zoltan M. Szaz, Germany's Eastern Frontiers (Chicago:  Henry Regnery Company, 1960), pp. 127-31. Also, The New York Times, August 3 and 30, 1945.

36. Rhode and Wagner, op. cit., p. 257.

37. Rzeczpospolita, November 30, 1946.

38. Wlodzimierz T. Kowalski, Polityka Zagraniczna RP, 1944-1947 (Warszawa:  Polski Instytut Spraw Miedzynarodowych, 1971), p. 11.

39. The New York Times, March 25, 1946.

40. The New York Times, July 26, 1946.

41. The New York Times, August 6, 1946.

42. The New York Times, September 7, 1946.

43. The New York Times, September 3 and November 11, 1946.

74

44. The New York Times, October 1, 1946.

45. The New York Times, April 16, 1949.

46. Lesniewski (ed.), op. cit., p. 31.

47. F. J. Schmitt (ed.), Im Deutschen Bundestag, Deutschland-und Ostpolitik 1 (Bonn: Pfattheicher & Reichardt, 1973), pp. 1-7.

48. Ibid., pp. 65 and following.

49. Michal Hoffmann, "O Niemcy Pokojowe, Demokratyczne i Zjednoczone," Nowe Droji, No. 4 (1952), p. 63.

50. The New York Times, December 29, 1956.

51. Lesniewski (ed.), op. cit., p. 140.

52. The New York Times, March 26, 1959.

53. The New York Times, August 12, 1960.

54. Janusz Sobezak, "Polityka Wschodnia SPD (Part II)," Sprawy Miedzynarodowe, No. 2 (1969), pp. 54 and following.

55. Josef Korbel, "West Germany's Ostpolitik: A Policy Toward the Soviet Allies," Orbis, No. 14 (Summer 1971), pp. 339-40.

56. Jerzy Sulek, "Organizacje Przesiedlencze a 'Nowa Polityka Wschodnia NRF,'" Sprawy Miedzynarodowe, No. 6 (1968), pp. 35 and following.

57. German Polish Dialogu. Letters of the Polish and German Bishops and International Statements (Atlantic-Forum, New York, 1966), pp. 18 and 25.

58. F. J. Schmitt (ed.), Im Deutschen Bundestag. Deutschland-und Ostpolitik 2 (C. Bertelsmann Verlag, Bonn, 1973), p. 35.

59. Trybuna Ludu, February 26, 1967. Also, Leon Kulczynski, "Granice Uprzejmosci Kurta--Georga Kiesingera," Nowe Drogi, No. 4 (1967), pp. 24-27 and 59.

60. Wladyslaw Gomulka, "Znaczenie Miedzynarodowych Ukladow z CSRS, NRD, i Bulgaria oraz Konferencji w Karlowych Warach," Nowe Drogi, No. 6 (1967), p. 41.

61. Der Spiegel, February 27, 1967.

62. Tarance Prittie, Konrad Adenauer, 1876-1967 (Tom Stacey, London, 1972), p. 236.

63. The New York Times, August 13, 1970.

64. Willy Brandt, A Peace Policy for Europe (Holt, Reinehart and Winston, New York, Chicago, San Francisco, 1969), p. 110.

65. Trybuna Ludu, May 18, 1969.

66. Schmitt (ed.), op. cit., pp. 245-6.

67. The New York Times, July 24, 1970.

68. The New York Times, November 4, 1970.

69. The Treaty Between the Federal Republic of Germany and the People's Republic of Poland (published by the Press and Information Office of the Federal Government, 1971), p. 8.

70. Lawrance L. Whetten, Germany's Ostpolitik; Relations Between the Federal Republic and the Warsaw Pact Countries (Oxford University Press, London, 1971), p. 163.

71. The Basic Law of the Federal Republic of Germany (German Information Center, New York, 1961).

72. Die Zeit, January 21, 1973.

73. Mieczyslaw Rakowski, "A Year Later," Polish Perspectives, No. 2 (1972), p. 8.

74. Quoted in The New York Times, November 19, 1970.

75. Jozef Winiewicz, "A New Chapter," Polish Perspectives, No. 2 (1971), p. 31.

76. The Treaty . . ., op. cit., pp. 13-15.

77. The New York Times, November 17, 1970.

78. Karl W. Deutsch, Gebhard L. Schweigler, Lewis J. Edinger, "Foreign Policy of the German Federal Republic," in Roy C. Macriolis (ed.), Foreign Policy in World Politics (Prentice-Hall, Inc., Englewood Cliffs, New Jersey, 1972), p. 135.

79. The Basic Law, op. cit.

80. The New York Times, December 7, 1970.

81. Brandt., op. cit., p. 152.

# 3
# Recovery

## Sovietization

A period of detente between the Polish government in exile and the Soviet Union followed the signing in London of the Polish-Soviet Pact in July, 1941, and the Moscow visit of Sikorski in December, when Stalin and the Polish leader agreed to a Declaration of Friendship and Mutual Assistance. But relations were restrained by the unresolved question of Poland's eastern border, and further magnified by the Soviet chicanery of a newly organized Polish Army, which in fear of repressions was evacuated to Persia to join the British instead of fighting on the Russian front. The final blow to these relations was the Katyn affair, that is, the massacre of Polish officers who had been taken prisoner by the Red Army when the Soviets invaded Poland in 1939. Once the Germans had announced their knowledge of the mass grave at Katyn forest, and the Soviets had denied responsibility for the deaths, the Poles requested a neutral Red Cross investigation. The Russians reacted by suspending diplomatic relations with the London Poles.

Following the break in relations in 1943, Polish Communists who had taken refuge in Moscow were ordered by Stalin to organize themselves as the Union of Polish Patriots and to form Polish military units. (Most of these people were not ethnically Polish; they were, in fact, to become known by their countrymen as the "Moscovites.") From Moscow came the charges that the London Poles had no mandate from the Polish People, that they were unwilling to fight for recovery of the Western territories the Germans had seized, that they favored repression of the left-wing parties and that they had collaborated with the Nazis by asking for an investigation of the Soviet crimes. Stalin's intentions were plain. He was calling into question the legitimacy of the Sikorski government and he was signalling both that further cooperation with the London Poles was impossible and that ultimately Poland's fate was to be decided in Moscow. Without the Communists, he was saying, the Polish nation would have no one to voice its interests.

Almost simultaneously another miniature group of Communists in Poland (the "Natives") proclaimed the establishment of a national parliament--the Home National Council--to demonstrate the democratic inclinations of the Left and to create an administrative cadre immediately available once Poland was free of the German occupation.

As soon as the Soviets crossed the Curzon Line, the Union of Polish Patriots reconstituted itself as the Polish Committee of National Liberation, and on July 22, 1944, it issued the Manifesto of the Committee of National Liberation, a document intended to provide the foundation for the shape of post-war Poland. The document stated that the Home National Council represented all the major (but unspecified) democratic political parties in Poland and abroad. It claimed also that the Council was the "sole legal source of authority in Poland" and that the Committee was assuming control of the Polish Army organized in the Soviet Union. Next, the Manifesto declared that the Home National Council and the Polish Committee of National Liberation were "acting on the basis of the Constitution of March 17, 1921, the only legally binding constitution that has been legally adopted." Thus, the emigre "government" in London and its delegates in Poland were described as exercising "usurped authority, illegal authority." Furthermore members of the Polish government in London were accused of impeding the struggle with Nazi Germany after having pushed Poland to catastrophe in 1939 with their bankrupt policies.

Also, the Manifesto assured that the future Polish state would be "free, strong, independent, sovereign and democratic," comprised of all Poles except the "Hitlerite agents" and those who had betrayed Poland in September, 1939. Finally, for the sake of popularity among the Polish peasants, the document pledged that agrarian reform would be carried out immediately.(1)

The circumstances surrounding the so-called Chelm manifesto have been described in an unpublished account written by Edward Osobka-Morawski, the first premier of the Polish People's Republic. According to Osobka-Morawski, in May, 1944, Stalin summoned to Moscow representatives of the Union of Polish Patriots and the Home National Council to discuss "creation of a nucleus of popular government." The delegates appeared in the Soviet capital on May 16 and after two months of debate decided to form the "Delegation of the Home National Council for the Liberated Territories." On July 19, they advised Molotov of their intentions. Molotov agreed with the proposed structure of the executive committee (four Communists, three Socialists, three from the peasantry and one independent), but he suggested a different name. His notion was to "borrow" a name from the French Communists who were organizing "Committees of National Liberation" to fight the Germans. Two days later, on July 20, the Poles accepted Molotov's proposal and after two more days they set up the Committee--not on Polish territory in Chelm, but in Moscow, the Soviet capital.

The government in exile responded with a policy of faits accomplis. The underground forces--the Home Army--were in-

structed to liberate Polish territories as they could.  Two
major cities in eastern Poland--Wilno and Lwow--were taken in a
joint Polish-Soviet operation.  Following their victory, however, units of the Home Army were overpowered by the Soviets and
were forced to join the Polish Army under the orders of the
Union of Polish Patriots.  The alternatives were execution or
imprisonment.  Some 50,000 Polish soldiers perished.(2)

A much more tragic experience lay ahead, the Warsaw
Uprising.  In July, 1944, the Red Army approached Warsaw and it
was expected that the Soviets would take the capital at any
time.  To preempt the Soviets, leaders of the Polish underground
moved to liberate the city before the Soviets could.  The
political aim was to establish the government in exile in the
Polish capital.  Up to that time the exiles had control of no
Polish territory.  Shortly before the uprising, delegates of the
Polish government who were in hiding in Poland received promo-
tions to ministerial posts and were authorized to assume
political control whenever military conditions permitted.  They
were to keep the pro-Soviet group from advancing to Warsaw.(3)

Left with no substantial military assistance from outside,
the uprising collapsed, taking with it any hope of sparing
Poland from Communist rule.  The cost was enormous:  200,000
dead, including the flower of the Polish intelligentsia, and the
destruction of 97 percent of the city.  Soviet units deployed
just across Vistula withheld support from the Home Army,
allowing the Nazis five months to eliminate anti-Soviet opposition in Poland.(4)

Once this last impediment had been removed, on December 31,
1944, the Home National Council issued a resolution transforming
the Polish Committee of National Liberation into the Provisional
Government.  Full international recognition of the new regime
was greatly facilitated by Western endorsement of Molotov's
proposal of adding ". . . to the Provisional Polish Government
some democratic leaders from Polish emigre circles" so as to
form a government of national unity.(5)  Subsequently, five
ministers of the exiled government were invited to join the
Provisional Government.  This group included Premier Stanislaw
Mikolajczyk, who became second vice premier in the new government.  This change, however, did not alter the Communist profile
of the regime, since most of the sixteen ministerial posts,
including police, defense and economy, were retained by recruits
from the pro-Soviet groups.

At this point Poland was ready for formal entry into the
international community.  The United Nations Conference in San
Francisco "reserved" a place in the charter for Poland and, when
on July 5, 1945, the United States and Great Britain recognized
the Warsaw regime, Poland was able to join the United Nations as
a co-founder.(6)

By the end of the war, Poland had lost more than six
million dead, the highest proportion of losses of any nation
involved in the conflict.  About four million Poles had emigrated or were left in Soviet Russia.  Half the country's prewar
territory had been seized by the Soviets.  The material losses
reached 40 percent of the national wealth, or some 50 billion

dollars.(7) Moreover, under the new arrangements, the government, the social and economic system and the territorial configuration had been designed without the participation of the people affected.

The irony of the situation was that while they were tailoring a government for Poland, the Big Three officially proclaimed that they had no authority to do it, since "free and unfettered" elections were to offer the Polish people the opportunity to make their own choice.

The idea of free elections was to some extent a convenient face-saving arrangement for the Western Powers, a useful defense against any accusations that Poland was "given away" to the Soviets. As for Moscow, it had little to fear from the outcome of elections in a country occupied by the Red Army and run by the Soviet-controlled secret police; in fact, elections they were bound to win could only enhance the legitimacy of the Warsaw regime. And for the Communists in Poland, they considered their determination to hold power—whatever the means—not as an act of base self-interest but as the only realistic way of preserving the nominal independence of the Polish nation.

Officially, the new Polish government was a five-party coalition including the Polish Workers Party, the Polish Socialist Party, the Peasant Party, the Democratic Party and the Christian Labor Party. The Polish Workers Party was composed of two groups of Communists: the Moscovites, representing the former Union of Polish Patriots, and the Natives, recruited from the former Home Council. The Socialists, who before the war enjoyed a limited popularity, were already dominated by the Communists. The same was true of the Democratic Party and of the Peasant Party, which was formed by the Communists and was given the same name as the authentic Peasant Party headed by Stanislaw Mikolajczyk. The Christian Party was promptly dissolved to prevent its development as a powerful representative of Poland's Catholics.

But, when Mikolajczyk returned to Poland he organized his movement into the reconstituted Polish Peasant Party, and resisted the provisional government's proposal for a single-ticket election, a device by which the distribution of seats would be determined in advance, much to the disadvantage of Mikolajczyk and his supporters.(8) And confident of his popularity, Mikolajczyk made a set of demands that included 70 percent of the seats in parliament for his party and the abolition of the Ministry of Public Security, the Polish branch of the Soviet NKVD.

His ambitions were plainly unacceptable to Moscow and because of that he was frequently accused of being ignorant of Poland's geography: Soviet Russia, not Britain or the United States, was Poland's neighbor. Indeed, Mikolajczyk was overlooking the fact that a political program for Poland could not be formulated without taking into account the international setting.

Meantime, the Communist authorities blamed the Polish Peasant Party for the continuing activities of the anti-Communist underground movement, the implication being that the

Peasant Party had become an "anti-democratic and fascist group."(9)  Another accusation aimed at Mikolajczyk was that he had violated an understanding reached in April, 1945, in Moscow, by organizing an additional political party in Poland.  According to the Communists, this undermined the unity achieved among the parties representing workers, peasants and the intelligentsia, the groups comprising the governmental bloc.  A consequence, the Communists feared, could be fratricidal struggle, providing the Soviet Union with a pretext for military intervention.  This was at a time when the Communists were stepping up the use of terror tactics.

This policy, designed to intimidate pro-Western political forces in Poland, included also a national referendum on unicameral parliament, nationalization of basic industries, and the endorsement of Poland's claim to the Oder-Neisse Line.(10)  It was a communist show of strength.  The secret police fabricated popularity, and exposed Mikolajczyk's inabilty to check the descent of the Soviet system in Poland.  Yet, despite the defeat, Mikolajczyk persisted in demanding an absolute majority of seats in parliament in exchange for his participation in the governing coalition.  Such attitude left the Communists with no choice but to suppress Mikolajczyk's party and to do it in the name of patriotism.  The "free and unfettered" elections in Poland were finally conducted in 1947.  On January 7, the provisional government announced it had gained a resounding victory over Mikolajczyk's opposition by winning no less than an 87 percent majority.(11)  The Soviet Union immediately certified that election procedures were as prescribed by the Yalta and Potsdam agreements.  Simultaneously, the Soviets also declared that the Oder-Neisse line was the "permanent" border between Germany and Poland.(12)

The West protested, but did not withdraw diplomatic recognition from the Warsaw regime, fearing such a step would encourage the Soviets to convert Poland into a Soviet republic. Poland nevertheless became isolated from the West, and nothing could prevent the nightmare of Stalinism.  The first stage of Sovietization, known as the United Front phase, was over, and Poland was facing something akin to its life under the Nazi occupation.  Although it appears that Mikolajczyk's willingness to compromise might have preserved a multiparty system in Poland, it is very unlikely that any independent political movement had much chance of surviving the next stage of Soviet domination.

Following the January elections Poland headed rapidly toward a system of one-party rule, patterned like so much in that period on the Soviet experience.  Mikolajczyk fled the country, and the peasant movement he abandoned was promptly "unified" with the Peasant Party, a puppet organization.  The newly established United Peasant Party, together with another marionette, the Democratic Party, came under the manipulation of the Communists as part of a multiparty charade.(13)  Then, as expected, once the organized peasant opposition ceased to exist, the time came to eliminate the Socialists, who were the last obstacle to an absolute Communist monopoly of power.  Over the vigorous oppositions of many Socialists, the Socialist Party was merged in September, 1948, with the Poland Workers Party to form the Polish United Workers' Party.(14)  This marked the end of the last political movement in Poland to enjoy genuine popular support.

The Polish regime was not even a minority government.  It was a political authority with no organic relationship to the people subject to its power.  In fact, the pattern of relations between the government and the governed resembled that of conquerors to the conquered.

This fact became even more evident when, after opposing the founding of the Cominform in 1948, the first secretary of the Polish Workers' Party, Wladyslaw Gomulka, was accused of Tito-ism--that is, of rightist and nationalist "deviation"--and was removed from his post.  The Moscovite faction prevailed over the ethnically national Communists who historically distinguished themselves as advocates of an independent Polish state.

Soviet conquest of Poland was completed when, at the end of 1949, Konstantyn Rokossowsky, marshal of the Soviet Union, arrived in Warsaw to assume the post of Polish Minister of Defense and was immediately made a member of the Politburo of the Polish Communist Party.

The regime moved decisively to remodel Poland according to Soviet design.  This meant not only the concentration of power in the hands of a few whose devotion to Stalin was unquestioned, but the rapid development of heavy industry and the forceful collectivization of agriculture.  The isolation of Poland's economy from the West was formalized when the country was required to withdraw its application for aid under the Marshall Plan and subscribe to the Molotov Plan, whose purpose was to integrate the economies of Eastern Europe into the Soviet system.(15)  By the end of 1949, the structures of the Molotov Plan were elaborated to become a Council of Economic Assistance (CEMA), which strengthened Soviet economic hegemony over the region.

In the official view, Polish authorities compared the Marshall Plan unfavorably with the Soviet program of economic aid.  The Russian project, they noted, based itself on the principles of "equality and mutual interest, (with) the Soviet Union promoting the interest of other nations which decided to take part in its economic organization."  In contrast to this, the Poles considered the United States was attempting with its proposal to limit the sovereignty of the client countries.  The final argument against the Marshall Plan was that its purpose was to enhance the capitalistic system at precisely the time when mankind was engaged in the process of the "curtailment of capitalism and the growth and expansion of socialism."(16)

Intensive Sovietization was also reflected in the Consti-tution that was adopted in 1952 after a nationwide "discussion." The country henceforth would be known not as the Republic of Poland, but as the Polish People's Republic.  The Constitution declared further that:

> . . . the basis of the people's power in Poland today
> is the alliance between the working class and working
> peasants. In this alliance, the leading role belongs
> to the working class--the leading class of the people,
> the class based on the revolutionary gains of the
> Polish and international working class movement, and
> on the historic experience of victorious socialist
> construction in the Union of Soviet Socialist Repub-
> lics, the first state of workers and peasants.(17)

With the coming of the 1950s, Poland's situation appeared
bleak. Nominally independent, the country was under such tight
Russian control that virtually no difference could be discerned
between its status and that of a Soviet republic. Rokossowski's
presence was a symbol of yet another national tragedy as it
became clear that "friendship" with the Soviet Union would leave
room for little that was Polish in post-war Poland.

During this period of frontal assault on Polish institutions and values, there was still one essential component of
national identity beyond the ability of the Communists to
destroy--the Roman Catholic Church. To comprehend the power of
the church in Poland it is necessary to realize that even the
Nazis avoided excessive confrontation with it, a pattern the
Communists were to follow. The regime anticipated antagonism in
its relations with the church, but it was unwilling to use
drastic means for fear of provoking a general uprising.

The campaign against the church was triggered in April,
1947, by a declaration Pius XII addressed to the German people
in which the pope implicitly condemned Poland for annexing the
Oder-Neisse territories and explicitly condemned the expulsion
of the Germans who lived there. The declaration stated that
regardless of the magnitude of the Nazi crimes, the retribution
was too heavy and was directed against the innocent. "Are the
victims of the countermeasure not in an overwhelming majority
human beings who had no part in the wartime crimes or who had no
influence upon them?" asked the pontiff. "Was this retaliatory
measure politically sensible and economically justified when one
considers the living necessities of the German people and the
well-being of Europe?"(18)

Up to that time, the Polish church had never expressed an
official opinion on the post-war territorial changes, but it
could no longer remain silent. The choice was difficult. In
the end, patriotism prevailed over loyalty to the Vatican, and
the Polish church assumed a position in support of the regime,
stating that Poland had historical, moral and political arguments to substantiate its claim on the Oder-Neisse territories.
In its statement, the Catholic episcopate of Poland directly
challenged the pope's declaration, affirming that the expulsion
of the Germans was an act of historical and moral justice;
regardless of how rough it was, it could in no way match the
crimes committed against the Polish nation by the Nazi
regime.(19)

Later, in 1950, when the government and the Polish episcopate concluded an "agreement" regulating the status of the
church in Communist Poland, three of the provisions read:

> (3) The Polish episcopate affirms that economic,
> historical, cultural and religious rights as well
> as historical justice demand that the Regained
> Territories belong to Poland forever.  On the
> understanding that the Regained Territories are a
> part of the Republic of Poland, the episcopate
> will address a request to the Holy See asking
> that the church administrations enjoying the
> rights of resident bishoprics be changed into
> permanent bishoprics.
> (4) The episcopate will as far as possible
> oppose activities hostile to Poland, particularly
> anti-Polish and revisionist activities on the
> part of the German clergy.
> (5) The principle that the pope is the authori-
> tative and supreme authority of the church
> relates to matters of religion, morality and
> church jurisdiction, but in other matters the
> episcopate will be guided by Polish raison
> d'etat. (20)

Thus, the church endorsed Poland's claim to the Oder-Neisse
territories and expressed a willingness to support the regime in
its efforts to gain permanent international recognition of the
new frontier.

This, however, did not prevent persecution of the church,
nor did it deter the regime from repeated attempts to sap the
social base of the church by portraying its clergy as an instrument of an anti-Polish Vatican.  But the Polish clergy has
always represented national interest, they were, as a matter of
fact, much more patriotic than the authorities, and consequently, the anti-church activities served only to enhance the
reputation of the church as a martyr of Communist persecution.
Paradoxically, during the Stalinist period in Poland, the Communist forces were more easily able to eliminate their allies than
they were their most formidable rival whose survival and
strength succeeded in preserving ideological pluralism in
Poland.

## National Communism

The de-Stalinization initiated by Nikita Khrushchev had broad international repercussions. In Poland it had the effect of undermining the legitimacy of the Moscovites who had been thrust into power thanks to Stalinist backing. They were now uncomfortably face to face with the Polish nation. Out of desperation, they promptly released Wladyslaw Gomulka from prison while Rokossowski returned to Moscow. Thus began a process of the nationalization of communism in Poland.

Gomulka's return to the post of first secretary of the Polish United Workers' Party had become possible because of the blow to the Moscovites' authority by Khrushchev's anti-Stalin campaign as well as by their inability to fulfill popular expectations. The Moscovites faced bankruptcy when Moscow stopped backing them as firmly as before, and the so-called "liberals" in the Communist Party (primarily former Socialists) began to accumulate power at the expense of the "conservatives." On the eve of October, the split in the Polish party became so deep that it paralyzed the party's everyday administrative functions, not to mention political leadership.

Wladyslaw Gomulka appeared as almost a neutral candidate for the senior party position and because of this he was acceptable to both factions. He did, however, seem to side with the liberals when he endorsed a moderate political and economic program advanced by that faction. At the same time, he sought popularity outside party channels, a well calculated maneuver to avoid being cast as a figurehead since he could count on the support of only a handful of his colleagues. Neither the Moscovites, the Socialists (the "liberals"), nor the so-called Partisans, who had spent the war in Poland fighting the Nazi occupiers, were impressed by the prospect of his leadership. Gomulka belonged to the small group of so-called Natives, the Communists who did not emigrate to Moscow in 1939.

The weakness of his position within the party was evident in 1948 when he was divested of his post as first secretary without any difficulty. In 1956, Gomulka decided to compensate for the uncertainty of party support by successfully appealing to the population at large with the help of liberal and national istic slogans. His acquisition of popularity had a two-fold effect: It increased his prestige inside the party and when the time came it helped convince Khrushchev that military intervention in Poland would be very costly.

Once reelected first secretary, Gomulka became a national hero practically overnight by announcing a program of democratization, promising greater popular participation in national and local decision-making, liberation of political control and rapid implementation of economic reforms.

To the Soviets, Poland had embarked upon a revisionist path. The danger of Soviet military invasion was imminent and only last-minute talks between Khrushchev and Gomulka averted what would have been the ultimate national disaster. The Soviet leadership reluctantly reconciled itself to the idea of a Polish road to socialism, a prospect that would have been out of the question in the preceding period. It did, however, gain assurances that there would be no tampering with the two essential pillars of the Soviet system: the monopolistic rule of the Communist Party and membership in the Warsaw Pact.

Thus Gomulka began a 14-year tenure as leader of Poland by making two contradictory commitments: self-government for the Poles, and ideological conformity to the Russians. In this uneven struggle, Moscow prevailed, as it had so many times before, and the period of Gomulka's rule was to be characterized by a step-by-step retreat from the ideas of October, so that by the mid-1960s he had become one of the most hard-headed and pro-Soviet leaders in the Soviet bloc.

Poland's economic predicament demanded instant attention, especially the agricultural sector ruined by collectivization. Reprivatization of farmland had in effect decentralized this sector of the national economy. But far more important were the reforms in industry.

A group of economic specialists headed by Oscar Lange proposed to decentralize planning and increase the autonomy of industrial managers, giving them direct control over production and distribution. They recommended a simplification of a bureaucracy overburdened by a double system of administration--party and government--and argued that the proper role of the party apparatus on either the central or local level should be to provide managers with general guidelines, instead of duplicating the managers' work. The party's capacity to dominate the national economy would not be impaired, the experts argued, while efficiency and productivity would be increased and administrative burdens would be vastly reduced.(21)

Parallel to economic decentralization was a proposal for enhanced worker control. Gomulka initially supported the idea of self-governing Workers' Councils but before long withdrew his backing so that these institutions became another bureaucratic appendage under the control of the party.

Instead of economic liberalism, the government reiterated its adherence to the principle of "democratic centralism." The Communists feared economic reform. Gomulka explained:

> In practice, the adoption of Lange's draft would have
> meant relinquishing party control of the country's
> economic life and, in the long run, losing control of
> political life . . . You can easily imagine what
> would have happened among our colleagues at the local
> level if they were suddenly told that there was no
> need for them to go to the places of production, that
> they had nothing to do but organize May Day meetings .
> . . We would have been forced to dismiss thousands of
> activists. Most of the party's economic apparatus
> would have had to be abolished. (22)

In this way, Gomulka kept his promise to Khrushchev that the Soviet model in Poland would suffer only minor cosmetic changes. Instead of economic reforms, Gomulka based his program of economic development on two foundations, both of them uncertain.

The regime decided to exercise its newfound autonomy in the expectation that further industrialization could be paid for by the private agricultural sector whose task it was to produce not only for the domestic market but to provide exports to Western Europe and the United States. In addition to coal, agricultural products such as meat, eggs and bacon became major exports, earning hard currency for the purchase of sophisticated machinery and equipment needed to sustain a high rate of industrial development. Agricultural output became a key factor in the economy. Ultimately the economic stability of Poland was to become dependent on American supplies of agricultural products, which in turn were contingent on Soviet-American relations.

Poland also requested considerable United States aid. For starters, Warsaw asked for $300 million, of which $200 million was to be used for the purchase of surplus farm commodities (wheat, fodder and cotton) paid in zlotys at market prices. The other $100 million was to be in the form of a loan provided by the Export-Import Bank to finance the purchase of machinery in the United States. The point was made that unless aid of that magnitude was forthcoming American credits would not be worth considering in view of possibly reprisals from the Soviet Union. Only substantial help with no political conditions attached could justify the risk.

The United States, however, had its hands tied by a provision of the Battle Act which specifically restricted material aid to regimes with military ties to the Soviet Union. The only assistance the Eisenhower and Kennedy administrations were able to provide was limited aid in the form of agricultural products; credits for machinery were reduced to a minimum and cut entirely in 1959. Between June, 1957, and February, 1963, Poland received aid in the amount of $637 million, with $519 million of this in agricultural commodities.(23)

Although it was less than hoped for, this American support of Poland's economy was significant. It boosted industrial development in an indirect way since the Poles did not have to enter the hard-currency markets to finance agricultural products for domestic consumption. It also permitted an increase in the export of meat to Western Europe and a relatively high rate of industrial growth in 1957 and 1958 was achieved without serious austerity at home. The United States was paying for what otherwise would have had to have been taken from domestic consumption.

TABLE I

Dynamics of Gross Industrial Production
in Poland (1956-1970) (24)

| | Previous Year = 100 | 1950 = 100 |
|---|---|---|
| 1956 | 109 | 231 |
| 1957 | 110 | 253 |
| 1958 | 110 | 278 |
| 1959 | 109 | 304 |
| 1960 | 111 | 338 |
| 1961 | 110 | 372 |
| 1962 | 108 | 404 |
| 1963 | 105 | 426 |
| 1964 | 109 | 466 |
| 1965 | 109 | 508 |
| 1966 | 108 | 545 |
| 1967 | 108 | 587 |
| 1968 | 109 | 642 |
| 1969 | 109 | 701 |
| 1970 | 108 | 708 |

Moscow viewed with great suspicion any method of building socialism that involved redistribution of the land to individual farmers and economic relations with the United States. Moreover, Gomulka permitted private investment in small enterprises which were running notorious deficits when under state administration. Adding to Soviet misgivings was the distribution of Poland's foreign trade; 60 percent with countries of the Communist bloc, but 40 percent with the rest of the world.

Of all these developments, the most annoying to the Soviets was Poland's request for American economic assistance. It suggested the inferiority of the Soviet model of development and the inability of the Soviet Union to provide its client states with all the necessities. Other members of the Communist bloc, unable to obtain such help themselves, were envious of Poland's demarche. Pravda felt obliged to reprimand both Gomulka and Tito, asserting that "the imperialists do not give anything to anyone for nothing. Everybody knows that American aid . . . leads in one form or another to economic and political dependence."(25)

Khrushchev's irritation reached a peak when, a few months after agreeing to forgive 2.4 billion rubles worth of Polish debt, he was presented with a bill from Gomulka for 300 million rubles ($75 million) for the transit of troops and supplies across Polish territory since the end of the war. At the same time, Moscow was informed that coal exports to the Soviet Union were to be reduced, and that Poland required an increase in Soviet raw materials, primarily iron ore.(26)

Furious, Khrushchev exploded at the Polish delegation, accusing it of trying to "milk" the Soviet Union. Referring to the American credits, Khrushchev advised the Poles to look for other sources of economic assistance. In retaliation, the Russians deliberately delayed scheduled deliveries of grain and no credits were made available to Poland until the middle of 1962.(27)

This economic harassment was followed by a campaign of sniping at Poland by the press of the other Soviet-bloc countries. It was initiated in Moscow by Izvestia, which implied that Poland had joined Yugoslavia on a dangerous revisionist path. The main source of revisionism was to be found in the policy of negating the leading role of the Soviet Union, the first socialist state, whose experience should always be assiduously copied. The Czechoslovakian press made similar accusations, stressing Poland's errors in agricultural policy (de-collectivization) and its unacceptable tolerance of intellectual dissent. The East Germans characterized Gomulka's return to power as the work of "imperialist moles." Even China joined this anti-Polish campaign, (28) calling Poland and Yugoslavia two revisionists in the socialist system.

Meantime, the situation at home began to deteriorate. The rapid pace of investment was accelerating inflationary tendencies in the Polish economy. Under such pressure, there were periodic price increases, mainly on vital necessities.

The political effects of these developments included a widening gap between the government and society--a reduction in Gomulka's ability to mobilize the population and counterbalance Soviet pressure.

A rapid increase in population also was having a negative effect on Polish living standards. Within thirty years, Poland's population grew from twenty-three million to thirty-four million. Immediately after 1956, Poland experienced an influx of repatriated Polish nationals from the Soviet Union. Though more people left Poland for the West than arrived from the East during this period, the new arrivals were much poorer than the Poles who emigrated. The over-all result was an additional burden on the government.

Reduction of world demand for coal and meat--Poland's principal exports--was another factor contributing to the emergence of new economic troubles. Because of a sharp drop in prices in 1958, a 20 percent increase in exports did not suffice to prevent a $200 million loss in planned income.(29) A foreign trade deficit was to become a permanent factor in Polish economic calculations. And the bill had to be paid by the consumer.

By the end of 1959, the economic situation was such that the regime began to question the wisdom of a policy that required balancing between Russia and America. The United States had been willing to supply Poland with agricultural commodities, but Poland could not obtain a long-term agreement necessary to stabilize this relationship. New negotiations had to be conducted annually and political issues were more often hampering solutions to purely economic matters. Although the United States did not attach any formal political conditions to its generous credits, it was expected that the Polish government would refrain from anti-American propaganda. U.S. aid was to encourage a policy of independence, but not to strengthen a member of the rival bloc.

Gomulka appreciated the economic importance of American credits, but he had to weigh their value against his country's security needs. West Germany and the United States refused to normalize relations with Poland and to recognize the Oder-Neisse line, leaving Warsaw no alternative but subservience to Moscow. In addition, Poland's economy was more dependent on Soviet supplies than on American trade. And lest he forget, unexpected movements of Russian troops in Poland were reminders to Gomulka that the danger of military intervention had not passed. Gomulka concluded that he could not risk another showdown with Khrushchev who had just defeated an "anti-party group" to become the more confident leader of the Soviet Union.

Adam Bromke explains that:

Gomulka clearly marked the limits beyond which he was not prepared to go in upholding Poland's right to her own road to socialism. As long as there existed some alternatives, which enabled him to digress from the Russian line without the impairing of ideological unity, he was willing to explore them. When pressed to the wall, however, he bowed to Moscow's will in the name of both Marxism-Leninism and political realism. (30)

At home there was renewed emphasis on discipline and ideological purity, raising fresh fears among peasants of forced collectivization. There were new attacks on the Catholic church and on intellectuals and increased restrictions on personal freedom. While Poland continued to be the most tolerant country in the Soviet bloc, nonetheless there was a clear retreat from the ideas of October. Soon the "spirit of October" was to become a historical issue.

Substantial growth in industrial production--58.8 percent within five years (1956-1960)--had very little meaning to the people whose income had increased only 5 percent. The average citizen had to spend between 60-70 percent of his salary on food. The standard of living was already low when the government announced that economic austerity was still ahead. Political withdrawal, general apathy and hopelessness returned.(31)

This pro-Soviet policy course terminated Polish-American detente. At first the government expected to improve its relations with the United States, agreeing to pay $40 million in compensation to American citizens whose property had been confiscated after the war, and to settle with Americans who held about $45 million in Polish bonds issued before the war.(32) It was the first case of a Communist-ruled country acknowledging such debts and being willing to repay them.

In December, 1960, Poland was given the last opportunity to earn hard currency on the American markets. The friendly and flexible Kennedy administration managed to persuade Congress to restore most-favored-nation status to Poland. On top of that, President Kennedy was granted the authority by Congress to use the hugh amount of Polish zloty kept in the American account to finance "projects of peace" in Poland--for example, construction of hospitals and schools.(33)

However, this sudden improvement in Polish-American relations took place a short time before another crisis in Berlin was staged by the Soviet Union, and a showdown developed between the superpowers over Cuba. In response to the Berlin crisis, the Polish government ordered the partial mobilization of its armed forces and declared its full support of Soviet policy in Europe. Later, ignoring the possibility of American retaliation, Poland signed a credit-barter agreement with Cuba to provide industrial goods in exchange for agricultural products and raw materials.(34) Under these circumstances, American aid of Poland, was actually an indirect subsidy to the Castro regime. These developments culminated with the visit of Minister Rapacki to Cuba: "the most expensive trans-Atlantic crossing since the Titanic."(35)

Polish-American relations deteriorated instantly. Congress imposed a ban on all foreign aid and trade with countries "known to be dominated by communism and Marxism," (36) depriving Poland of most-favored-nation status and cutting further deliveries of agricultural products. This last restriction was promptly modified and the president was granted discretionary power to decide each case individually. The administration quickly authorized $60 million worth of wheat for Poland, but it could not change a sense of disappointment among the Poles. The American move was also a blow to the liberals in the Polish communist Party who lost control over the Central Committee. Thus Poland, a pioneer of economic reform in the Soviet bloc, also became the first to criticize its purposefulness.(37)

In admitting to the seriousness of the economic problems the country faced, the government attempted to place the entire blame on the West, primarily America, as an unreliable trading partner. This important setback in Poland's foreign trade policy coincided with a decline in agricultural production at home, due in part to bad weather but also to the reticence of peasants alarmed by Gomulka's sharpened ideological rhetoric which raised fears of collectivization. Poland went through a rather serious economic crisis in 1963 when the rate of industrial growth had to be reduced by half, (38) and agricultural exports were sharply curtailed. At the same time, without American credits, Poland was forced to go into the hard currency markets to purchase wheat from Canada. The hope for prosperity was gone.

The economic failures combined with international tension to the advantage of the orthodox wing of the Polish Communist Party. Gomulka, though popular at the outset of his tenure, was never able to muster sufficient force to purge the party of the Stalinists. Not only did they survive the October revolt, by the beginnings of the 1960s they had resurfaced as the strongest faction in the party, pulling it toward conservative communism.

On top of an anemic economy, the regime's problems at home included the disobedience of intellectuals, the perpetuation of intraparty struggles and not the least of all, the non-conformist policy of the Catholic Church. One of the paradoxes of the Communists' post-war triumph in Poland was the almost unprecedented strengthening of the church. By making Poland a nationally homogeneous state, the Communists in effect eliminated all religious groups save the Catholics, who after the war constituted nearly all of society. Too weak to challenge the church directly, and unable to divide it into rival groups, the Communist regime chose a policy of formal accommodation with the Catholic hierarchy, while attempting to curtail the church's influence.(39)

Several anti-Catholic initiatives were organized during the pre-1956 period, but the policy was self-defeating since it only reinforced the impression of the church as a martyr to foreign-imposed Communist rule. Vindication of a nationalist orientation in the Communist Party was a triumph for the episcopate which had never collaborated with the Stalinist regime. In October, 1956, the nation welcomed the return from prison of both Wladyslaw Gomulka and Stefan Cardinal Wyszynski.

Among the first concessions make by Gomulka was a promise of religious toleration. A new agreement was concluded between the regime and the hierarchy which granted the church the right to appoint religious teachers paid by the state; religious instruction was to be conducted for believers in public schools; church property was to be respected and the Catholic University in Lublin, together with many seminaries, would be allowed to operate freely.(40)

Because of a need for popular acceptance, the Communists merely suspended the conflict. Within three years they were to return to a policy of harassment, using the Stalinist practices of heavy taxation, refusal to issue church construction permits, conscription of priests into the Army, prohibition of foreign travel and the cancellation of religious instruction in the public schools.(41) Fearing economic repercussions, the regime felt compelled once again to suspend the conflict, with the result that if there was a truce, it now was one without mutual trust. There followed a period of coexistence between the church and the regime, but it was one marked by competition and malice.

As in other East European countries, government policy was to promote a division within the clergy between the "priest patriots" and the "reactionary, pro-Vatican" hierarchy. The most urgent task, however, was to isolate Cardinal Wyszynski from the rest of the hierarchy. The 1966 celebration of the 1000th anniversary of Polish statehood and the introduction of Christianity into Poland became the occasion for a showdown. The church rejected an invitation from the government to combine the celebrations of the secular and religious millennium because it felt it would be placed in the position of appearing as a prop for communism. In any event, the fundamental purposes of the church and the regime were in sharp conflict. Cardinal Wyszynski stressed Poland's historical links with Western cultural tradition and emphasized the idea of reconciliation with Germany. After an exchange of letters between the Polish and German bishops, the millennium of Christianity in Poland was celebrated under the slogan, "We forgive."

"We don't forgive!" exclaimed government posters. Anti-West German propaganda intensified to the point of hysteria. The official government attitude toward the millennium cele-bration was an emphasis on the previous twenty-five years of Polish history--Communist rule, "friendship" with Russia and an abrasive policy toward the Catholic Church. For a while Gomulka seemed to lose his sense of restraint and launched an aggressive anti-clerical campaign including the organization of cele-brations at the same time as the Catholic festivities, cancel-lation of trains, unexpected registration of cars, a ban on foreign tourism, refusal to allow the pope to visit Poland, the falsification of the text of the letter written by the German bishops and the charge that the Polish bishops were willing to make territorial concessions to Germany.(42)

Again it was a self-defeating course of action. The false charges had to be disowned, attitudes toward West Germany soon had to be revised when the opportunity for an agreement with Bonn presented itself and Poles learned that it was the party itself--not the church--that was deeply split into factions, with Gomulka losing touch with reality.

Within days after the Polish-West German treaty of 1970, Gomulka, by now isolated from the nation by party bureaucrats, fell from power. The treaty marked another victory of the church, which was the first to advocate reconciliation. Cardinal Wyszynski appeared the more skillful politician. Better than the party leaders he showed a sharp perception of international developments and of the national mood. The authority and influence of the Catholic Church had been reaf-firmed. It was not the first time that the church was called on to assume a leading spiritual and political role in a nation so often deprived of its political identity.

The Catholic-Communist conflict in Poland could be reduced to the question of who was the better patriot. With his growing subservience to Moscow, Gomulka had antagonized the nationalist sentiments of the Poles, from which the church could only profit. Yet when Polish communism combined for a time with nationalism, the church was also the principal beneficiary. Under existing conditions, Catholicism and nationalism over-lapped to such an extent that separation had become unat-tainable. Gomulka attempted coercion and lost his duel with Wyszynski.

Another prestigious and influential group whose attitude was of concern to the regime was the creative intelli-gentsia.(43) Its members had supported Gomulka in October, 1956, but became progressively disaffected as the first secretary reversed the process of liberalization. Clashes involving the authorities with scholars and writers became frequent. The government found itself in an awkward position since the majority of the dissenters were trusted members of the party who enjoyed a great deal of political freedom and had easy access to classified information.

In 1956, the intellectuals credited Gomulka with sincerity in wanting liberalization and rule by consensus. He publicly guaranteed that his policies would be in tune with the basic desires of the Polish people, but indeed the last thing he wanted was democracy. Gomulka was an opportunist ready to use the slogans of freedom and liberalism to gain the popular support he needed to counterbalance pressure from Moscow. Eventually he was to pay a heavy price for this popularity obtained by cheap means. Disappointed intellectuals reacted spontaneously and vigorously, challenging the party by both direct and subtle methods. Gomulka was never able to bring them to heel.

Among the leading dissidents was Leszek Kolakowski. This brilliant Marxist became the most outstanding critic of dogmatic, orthodox, Soviet-style communism. He did not hesitate to question the wisdom or the "scientific nature" of Marxism-Leninism. Marxism, according to Kolakowski, should not be regarded as an ultimate achievement in philosophy and methodology--a universal system--but as a "separate school of thought (which) will gradually become blurred and ultimately will disappear entirely."

Another very unorthodox feature of Kolakowski's understanding of Marxism was his belief that "typical for Marx is . . . the tendency to emphasize those primary social divisions which are most influential in determining historical development" (44) and this conceptual framework did not lose its relevance for contemporary Communist societies.

Such "thoughtless" arguments were not welcomed by the "office"--the name Kolakowski used to characterize the party apparatus. The infallibility of Marxist-Leninist dogma had become a major point in the effort to make Communist rule legitimate. Consequently, Moscow attacked Gomulka for his tolerance of "revisionist" tendencies in the Polish Communist movement and Khrushchev warned that failure to liquidate "revisionism" might result in developments similar to those in Hungary.(45)

Gomulka promptly purged the editorial staff of the party organ, Trybuna Ludu, suppressed the youth weekly, Po Prostu, which in October, 1956, had been a leading platform for new ideas, and made changes on the editorial board of another journal, Nowa Kultura.(46) This was done, according to Gomulka, in the name of common sense.

Gomulka went on to defend the narrow self-interest of the ruling bureaucrats who feared Kolakowski's "Marxism," suggesting that in many ways it sounded like "irreligious Christianity" instead of an obedient glorification of party rule.(47) The regime imposed censorship and told the intellectuals bluntly that either they would contribute to Communist propaganda or they would face charges of slandering the Polish state. Still, only a few agreed to conform.

One of the best examples of a cautious and systematic criticism of the government was that of the Catholic deputies in parliament associated in a group called "Znak" (Sign). This small but influential organization was tolerated by the regime

which liked to preserve the facade of democracy.  For the Znak
people, participation in government affairs had become an
excellent opportunity to "transmit the opinion and demands of
the nation" to the regime.(48)  They assumed that the general
direction of political developments in the Communist countries
was toward democracy, and their ambition was to make Poland the
most progressive country in the Soviet bloc.

The Znak deputies never questioned premises the regime
considered fundamental, namely, the political leadership of the
party and "friendship" with the Soviet Union.  But when the
degree of political tolerance sharply diminished so did their
support for the regime.  Unlike many others, they employed
enough flexibility to survive Gomulka; this was possible,
however, because they adopted a more conformist attitude.

Disaffection of Polish writers surfaced dramatically in
1964.(49)  Thirty-four well known writers and scientists sent a
letter to Premier Jozef Cyrankiewicz protesting the "restrictions in allocation of paper for printing books and periodicals,
as well as tightening of press censorship."  This letter became
known as the "Freedom Manifesto."  According to the authors,
such a policy, if continued, would create "a situation dangerous
for the development of Polish national culture."  Moreover:

> The undersigned, recognizing that the existence of public
> opinion, the right to criticize, freedom of discussion and
> access to reliable information are necessary factors to
> progress, and being motivated by civic concern, demand that
> Polish cultural policy be changed to conform to the spirit
> of the rights guaranteed by the Polish Constitution and to
> the national good. (50)

Again the policy of attack and voluntary retreat followed.
First the authors of the letter were not allowed to publish or
to speak publicly, and restrictions on their foreign travel were
imposed.  Some of them had to face trials staged by the regime
for alleged dissemination of "false and slanderous information
about the country's internal situation."(51)

A few months later authorities began to reverse this trend.
Defendants were ordered released by Gomulka and were allowed to
publish again; paper was allocated and passports were issued.
No concessions, however, were made in the policy of censorship
and officially the importance of this issue was played down by
the regime.

Unlike leaders of some other Communist countries, Gomulka
was too weak to force a showdown with the intellectuals.  He
preferred to present himself as a benevolent leader and reaffirm
the principle of party control while avoiding a conflict that
could be exploited by his opposition within the party.  In
reality, however, restrictions were increased and the government
adopted a more orthodox attitude.(52)

In March, 1968, the entire intellectual community revolted.
The greatest purpose for the regime was the behavior of members
of the young generation, the products of Communist Poland, who
took to the streets to express their enmity for the system.

These idealistic youth were protesting the lack of imagination, the surfeit of bureaucratic inefficiency, widespread corruption and the regime's predilection for interpreting international developments strictly in terms of the Second World War. For the young, the so-called "German danger" was purely theoretical; the principal issue for them was the obvious discrepancy between officially advocated ideas and social reality. Young people lost patience waiting for the fulfillment of promises so generously made by the party.(53)

Members of the ruling clique regarded ideology as no more than an instrument for gaining or holding power and could not anticipate that it might become a strong source of inspiration to their more idealistic co-citizens. While conformism had been the dominant value for the old generation of Communists, the young Marxists valued freedom and social justice and were eager to inquire into the causes of recurring alienation. Polish youth fought the regime in the name of Marxism-Leninism so imaginatively that one student was arrested for reading a letter of Lenin's whose contents the authorities deemed inappropriate.(54)

The generation gap had become a fact, despite the refusal of the authorities to acknowledge it. The system and its ideology were too narrow to meet new demands. Quoting from a resolution prepared by the Council of the Philosophical Faculty of Warsaw University, Gomulka conceded that "the university youth movement developing outside the framework of official organizations has for the last four days been an authentic mass movement uniting the overwhelming majority of students of Warsaw University."(55) However, from those developments he drew quite a different and erroneous set of conclusions.

The revolt, the young people argued, had been directed against the growing servility toward the Soviet Union and "the control exerted by the international bureaucracy over the world Communist movement." The time had come for an "anti-bureaucratic revolution (which) will put an end to the dictatorship's control." Further, "the class interest of the workers demands the abolition of the bureaucratic ownership of the means of production and exploitation."(56)

Besides its strong ideological character, the March revolt had unmistakable nationalistic overtones. It was provoked by the decision, at Soviet request, to close down a performance of Dziady ("Forefathers"), a drama written by the greatest Polish romantic, Adam Mickiewicz. "This could be compared to a decision to ban Shakespeare in England," (57) Polish journalists explained. In fact, the authorities demonstrated their ignorance of Polish literature by their initial grant of permission to stage Dziady as the National Theater's part in celebrating the anniversary of the Bolshevik Revolution.

The audience reacted with spontaneous applause at the lines:

They make me free--where the news came from I do not know
But I know what freedom means if granted by Moscow
Scum, they will just take fetters off my hands and feet

But shackle the soul.

And:

No wonder we are being cursed here
A century has passed
Since Moscow has been giving Poland
Nothing but blackguards.

Students and intellectuals revolted demanding that the play be restored to the stage. The Union of Polish Writers in Warsaw protested, calling the decision "a flagrant example of unwarranted censorship."(58) Demonstrations took place in every academic center, but the slogans urging the tolerance of creative freedom found little understanding or support among the working people. The Polish intelligentsia saw itself as the ally of workers. It neglected, however, to establish a basis of communicating with them. The intellectuals' demands had nothing of an economic nature to them, making it easier for the authorities to isolate the intellectuals who were easily dispersed.

Another element contributing to the regime's uneasiness was the persistent power struggle among factions in the Communist Party.

Soon after the days of October and the population had returned to work, Gomulka, the newly reinstated first secretary, found it prudent to position himself in the party hierarchy between the liberals and the conservatives (Moscovites joined by the Partisans), ever vigilant against the possibility of any individual acquiring enough power to oust him. He worked to balance the political influence of both wings, making this a central feature of his leadership. This policy contributed to a certain stability, but an unwanted consequence of it was his eventual immobilism. The liberals proposed reforms, the conservatives defeated them, gaining an advantage in the struggle.(59)

Fresh arguments for a conservative orientation were supplied by the subservience to Moscow, the failure of Poland's Westpolitik, economic setbacks, conflicts with the church and the intellectuals. The choice actually was foreshadowed by Gomulka himself in March, 1959, during the Third Congress of the PUWP. Four years later, after the Fourth Congress, the liberals were cast as "revisionists," and the Stalinist faction emerged dominant on the Central Committee.(60)

The victory was temporary. The entire conservative wind felt under control of the politically ambitious Partisans. They cherished hard-line attitudes and had no cause for pride in their compulsory partnership with the Communists who had sat out the war in Moscow, returning the the Red Army in 1945 to relegate the Partisans to a subsidiary role in domestic security. The Partisans were not trusted by the Moscovites, and because of that they had to submit to the added humiliation of having Soviet agents, NKVD men, permeate their ranks until 1956. When Gomulka returned to power, the Partisans took advantage of the opportunity to organize themselves into a pressure group inside the party while their leader, General Mieczyslaw Moczar-- minister of Internal Affairs and a Central Committee member--

became hopeful that it was only a matter of time before he would have Gomulka's position.

Nationalism was a central element in the Partisans' political platform. This, after all, was the only group of Polish Communists which had actually fought the occupants and its members placed strong emphasis on Poland's own contribution to the defeat of the Nazis. This appeal was skillfully employed in propaganda to entice former soldiers of the Home Army to join the group.

The Union of Fighters for Freedom and Democracy (ZBOWiD), one of the Partisan's organizations, had served as a channel between the Security Police and society. Membership in ZBOWiD guaranteed preferential consideration in the distribution of social benefits. Ideology was ignored since the Leninist slogan, "He who is not with us is against us," was reversed: "He who is not against us is with us."(61)

The Partisans followed a policy of cautious maneuver until 1964 when Moczar began to pursue his political ambitions more energetically. He suffered a setback in mid-1965 when Gomulka removed him from command of the regime's military-political guard (the Corps of Internal Security--KBW) and appointed a friend, Marshal Marian Spychalski, in his stead.(62) The Partisans waited for an opportunity to stage a major provocation.

After the Six Day War in the Middle East, the Soviet Union and all of its East Bloc allies except Romania launched a vigorous propaganda campaign against Israel. In Poland, Moczar and his associates saw the chance to exploit the campaign for their own purposes. Their scheme called for the organization of demonstrations against the Russians and against the regime. The police were then to make selective arrests of students of Jewish ethnic origin whose parents had high party positions. This would "prove" that the "Zionist fifth column" had been operating inside the Central Committee and the government. A discredited Gomulka would have to resign, relinquishing power to Moczar.(63)

Moczar, however, failed to anticipate that Gomulka would welcome the anti-Semitic campaign because it would allow the first secretary to purge his opponents in the party. He turned Moczar's provocation to his own advantage, depriving Moczar of his victory. Gomulka moved against both liberals and conservatives in the party, the police (the Partisans), writers, scholars and even Catholic dissenters. He managed to disperse every group that posed a challenge to his power.

This general house cleaning ended in November, 1968, at the Fifth Party Congress. All the Communist groups, the "old guard" who had influenced politics since the end of the war, were in a state of disarray. Gomulka was left with few rivals but his sympathizers were fewer still, and he had to call on Leonid Brezhnev, the Soviet leader, to back him during the Congress. Brezhnev praised Gomulka as "a faithful son of the Polish working class (and) an outstanding leader of the international Communist movement."(64) Gomulka packed the newly elected Central Committee with young apparatchiks from the provinces, men he considered the least dangerous to him. His was a Pyrrhic

victory, though, and bad strategy. Gomulka had deprived himself
of a defense in case of a challenge from the bottom.

The principal factors which brought about Gomulka's down-
fall were the same as those which fourteen years earlier had
supplied him with the opportunity to ascend from prison to the
highest office in the country. He knew how to take political
advantage of his opponents' economic missteps, but he never
learned how to organize production on a sound basis or to
surround himself with men who could. Like Khrushchev, Gomulka
was a high stakes gambler who thrived on intrigue and theater.
But he hadn't much concern for the details of constructive work.
Throughout his tenure he spent his energy fighting various
elements of Polish society and above all political cliques in
the party. His efforts were for the purpose of personal power,
but they were cloaked in ideological purity or political real-
ism--fear of the Soviet Union, the ultimate guarantor of his
position. His ambition was no less than to gain for himself
recognition as the leading ideologue and international affairs
expert in the entire Soviet bloc. What Poland needed was an
able economic administrator. But like every Communist leader in
a "conspiratorial" post, Gomulka could not handle the non-
political aspects of economic issues.

Periodic price "regulations" characterized the last six or
seven years of Gomulka's rule. The authorities wanted to
decrease consumption of food--an important export item--and
increase the purchase of goods produced by domestic industry.
Food prices were increased and the official explanation was that
this was done to prevent people from exceeding the recommended
physiological level of meat consumption!(65) It was in their
own best interest.

Another feature of Gomulka's economic policies was an
attempt to improve "economic accounting at the central level."
Facing the choice of centralization, which guaranteed firm party
control at the expense of efficiency, or decentralization, which
would improve efficiency at the expense of political supervision, Gomulka naively expected that it was possible to have
both total control and high efficiency if only the central
decision-making process could operate more effectively. That,
in addition to partial reprivatization of restaurants and gas
stations (66), brought no significant improvement. Productivity
continued to decline.

Gomulka's routine response to some economic problems was to
cut domestic consumption of food so as to increase agricultural
exports. He tried this for the last time in December, 1970,
when he hoped "to gain several additional millions . . ."(67) by
raising prices on meat and flour just before Christmas. It was
the second consecutive bad harvest, the result of a severe
winter and heavy spring flooding. Food was not available in
sufficient amounts. Facing high demand just before the Christmas holiday, the authorities were reluctant to admit to the
shortages and made their fatal decision to raise prices. Timing
was no doubt a major factor that led to rioting.

A parallel cause of dissatisfaction was an official proposal to change the system governing wages. As a way of

increasing productivity, the government decided to introduce a system of incentives, in place of stable weekly salaries. Understandably, the workers feared that this measure would result in lower earnings for them.  In fact, Gomulka was breaking an unwritten social contract in Communist society, according to which the workers could count on guaranteed economic security.

The price and wage measures were perceived as provocations. Disturbances quickly exploded into widespread violence.  In his isolation, Gomulka was unable to see any reason for the strikes and riots other than an attempt to stage a "counterrevolution." He authorized the use of firearms.  More than 1,000 people were killed and several thousand were injured in the bloody repression that ensued.  Shooting failed to restore order and Gomulka lost control of both the party and the nation.  He was deserted by the armed forces when General Wojciech Jaruzelski, the defense minister, refused to send troops against the workers, and was informed by Moscow that the crisis must be solved by political means.  Unable to control the situation, Gomulka resigned.

Such was the forced departure of the first man to come to power with national support in the Soviets' East European empire.  Stubbornness was his prime political asset--it had helped him face down Khrushchev in 1956--but it also was a source of his inflexibility and lack of imagination.  And though he rose to power with national support and rallied the nation against the Soviets, he was to reverse that partnership, siding with Moscow against the nation when the time came.  He antagonized every possible social and political group in the country, and at the end even his Russian protectors found him cumbersome. Like Walter Ulbricht in East Germany, Gomulka had become an anachronism in the bloc; he was more orthodox than the Soviets.(68)

## Socialist Democracy

Succeeding Gomulka as first secretary, Edward Gierek came face to face with the ineluctable question of how to make the Communist system work.  In attempting to do so, Gierek operated with some advantages denied his predecessors, including an international climate of detente and an unprecedented lack of Soviet restrictions on Poland's pursuit of Western economic cooperation and assistance.  Due to the fruits of detente, he was the first postwar Polish leader who (because the dispute had been decided in Poland's favor) could not count on fabricating a national consensus behind his policies by manipulating the issue of the Oder-Neisse Line.

Under Gierek's leadership, Communist rule became openly justified by the proximity of Soviet power.  Gierek himself stated that Poland's relative independence, if not its right to exist, could be maintained only as long as the country was governed by a pro-Soviet Communist Party.  For this reason, Poland, he argued, was allied with the Soviet Union by "inseparable ties" and unconditional acceptance of this objective reality was the ultimate "proof of patriotism."  Thus Poland continued to function as a one-party state bound by links of "friendship" with Soviet Russia.

This message was directed to Moscow as well as to the Polish people.  By it, the Soviets were assured that Gierek and his "Silesian gang" were not reformers of the Dubcek type, but realists interested first of all in economic performance.  It also implied that the Soviets should respect Poland's autonomy so as to avoid an outburst of anti-Russian sentiment.

Gierek's credentials as party leader and Soviet loyalist passed scrutiny.  In Soviet eyes he was a less uncertain choice to succeed Gomulka than General Moczar, whose ambition gave them pause.  In addition, Gierek had worked as a miner for eighteen years in France and Belgium, thus making him the first (former) worker to head the Polish workers' party.  As a regional party leader in Silesia, he had gained a reputation for efficiency, pragmatism and open-mindedness and he was expected to introduce a degree of enlightenment to Communist absolutism in Poland.

Gierek was popular, something he found both flattering and useful, especially as leverage against Moscow.  In his criticism of Gomulka and his policies, Gierek declared the socialism should not be confused with the unrestricted development of heavy industry; the people's welfare must be its essence. Gomulka had committed grave mistakes, the new first secretary said, by neglecting popular demands and the former miner pledged that under his leadership the gap that separated the workers from their "vanguard" would disappear.

"The iron principle of our economic policy and our policy in general," Gierek said, "must be consideration of reality, broad consultation with the working class and intelligentsia, respect for the principle of collective leadership and democratization of intraparty and governmental structures."(69) Thus, Gierek pledged to keep the interests of the Polish people in focus, and to maintain, if not democracy, at least a constant

dialogue with the nation. He invited all Poles to participate
in political life by substituting a consultative system--which
he labeled socialist democracy--for the infamous and traditionally Leninist practice of democratic centralism.(70)
Gierek's socialist democracy should not be confused with the
Western concept of social democracy founded on the principle of
free elections. Rather it was intended simply to strike a
balance between the ideological aspirations of the Communist
Party and the demands of the Polish people, as long as Communist
hegemony and Soviet security were not jeopardized. Gierek's
democratization, it was asserted, would not mean strengthening
of party rule, but a meaningful step toward self-government.

It was a common-sense proposal, a cautious but significant
move in the right direction and within the limits of the one-
party system. A general impression was that the Poles had
learned a painful lesson and would not dare to provoke the
Russians. That this lesson had been absorbed became evident
during the revolt of 1970. Gierek publicly acknowledged the
"admirable political consciousness" on the part of the younger
generation which had been active in the uprising. It was a
hopeful sign, a great encouragement for a policy intended to
bring the nation and its rulers closer together.(71)

The December, 1970, events had a sobering effect on
Poland's Communist rulers. Their new attitude of paying closer
attention to national sentiments was apparent in their rejection
of the Soviet interpretation of the revolt. The Soviets characterized it, not as a spontaneous outburst of discontent with the
system, but as the result of a counterrevolutionary provocation
cooked up by a conspiracy of Kulaks and their children in the
shipyards together with the hierarchy of the Roman Catholic
Church.(72) By implication, the Soviets condemned Poland's
national path to socialism whose deviations included private
agriculture and a tacit partnership between the party and the
church.

By contrast, Gierek blamed the previous leadership for
creating economic conditions that fully justified the explosion.
The new leadership immediately cancelled the proposed 15-30
percent price increases in foodstuffs and proclaimed price
stability for two years, later extended it for an additional two
years, and allowed the freeze to endure in principle until the
martial law regime of December, 1981. Price stability became
the centerpiece of official propaganda and was seen as a key to
political stability. This policy forced the regime to extend
enormous subsidies to food production.

But it was a first sign that Gierek's ambition was to be a
leader in his own right, an ally but not a pawn of Moscow. The
obligatory friendship with the Soviet Union was to be a give and
take relationship designed to increase the number of political
and economic options available to the Polish Communists. Gierek
fully realized that Soviet support was no substitute for genuine
popularity at home. Gomulka, after all, had gained power over
Moscow's opposition and had lost it due to popular outrage. The
unconditional Soviet demand that Poland be governed by the

Communist Party does not require as a counterpart unconditional support for its individual leaders.

The entire decade of Gierek's leadership failed to yield the promised democratization in the sense of greater public participation in decision-making, but it undoubtedly brought about a considerable decrease in the political control of society. This widely perceived liberalization, however, was more a byproduct of the sharp and never-ending factional struggles within the party than it was a result of a deliberate policy of socialist democracy.

From its inception at the end of the Nineteenth Century, the Marxist movement in Poland was prey to intense nationalism and bitter factional struggles. In Gierek's case, matters were complicated by the invasion of the central party bureaucracy by his Silesian loyalists who were superimposed on the Warsaw cadres. In the capital, only General Moczar with his Partisan supporters assisted Gierek in the coup he executed during the disarray and confusion of the blood December events.(73) Gierek was a practical stranger in Warsaw where he had no solid roots. He was fully aware that the endorsement he received from Moczar was but a tactical prelude to Moczar's fullblown assault on the office of first secretary.

Moczar, however, was politically handicapped by the lack of Soviet confidence in him. His help in Gierek's palace revolution earned him a brief promotion to the Politburo and the Central Committee secretariat, an accumulation of responsibilities that made him the Number Two man in the regime. But this sudden rise was followed by an equally steep decline in his political fortunes, concluding with his demotion to a secondary post in the government outside the party hierarchy. His, in effect, was the last political battle fought by the then-aged veterans of the Polish Communist movement. A new generation of leaders was moving into position, gradually replacing the Moscovites, Natives and Partisans.

Gierek and his group of Silesians belonged to a group known as the technocrats, men who were less interested in matters of ideology than in administrative and economic efficiency. In Warsaw they encountered the united but not homogeneous resentment of the orthodox conservatives manning the central bureaucracy. The Polish Communist establishment was weakened by the effects of Gomulka's economic debacle and by a lack of nationally respected leaders to replace him. But it never lost its power to resist unwelcome effects of Gomulka's economic debacle and by a lack of nationally respected leaders to replace him. But it never lost its power to resist unwelcome political changes. Especially noteworthy in this group of neo-Stalinists were Premier Piotr Jarosziewicz and Foreign Minister Stefan Olszowski, both members of the Politburo who formed a counterweight to the technocrats. This group was successful in staving off even minor attempts to diminish the central control of the economy, a most essential reform.

The Soviets encouraged such "collective leadership" for it facilitated the exercise of their influence. Moscow followed the old imperial principle of divide et impera. Intraparty disputes prevent the monopolization of power by one individual who might then feel strong enough to oppose Moscow. Collective leadership and "family quarrels" create a need for constant Soviet involvement in the internal affairs of other parties, making Moscow the arbiter and assuring Soviet dominance. Surprisingly, Soviet methods closely resemble the way tsarist Russia skillfully manipulated Polish aristocrats in the Eighteenth Century to hinder their unity and prevent the implementation of necessary domestic reforms.(74)

The clique of hawks in the Polish Communist Party attracted considerable support within the party, especially among the numerous apparatchiki, whose chief characteristics were servility and a pathological fear of any reform which might render their services unnecessary. This group adopted a strategy of undermining the confidence Gierek enjoyed in Moscow. His opponents portrayed him as a Polish Dubcek, a revisionist capable of subverting the party's leading role by excessive tolerance of intellectuals and the church, as well as the advocate of a scheme to free Poland from dependence on the Soviet Union and COMECON by building ties to Western capital and markets.

As the Warsaw daily Zycie Waszawy informed its readers, "a sharp battle is taking place on many levels between the old and the new."(75) The Communist hardliners were gravely concerned about the new and dangerous image Gierek projected. With his rhetorical emphasis on consumerism and self-government, the first secretary more closely resembled the leader of a democratic nation than he did the trusted caretaker of Leninist dogma. There followed an unwelcome (for the hardliners) and dangerous (for the party) rise of popular expectations, making the party hostage to its own promises. Gierek was able to prevail as long as he did because of his popularity and the unwillingness of the Soviets to rock the boat in Poland.

At the outset, Gierek appeared to be a liberal, a pragmatist and a patriot.

First of all, he lifted direct censorship on two newspapers, Trybuna Ludu and Polityka, both representing the Central Committee of the PUWP. It was supposed to be the first step toward the complete elimination of censorship in the future. The lifting of censorship on the two papers was more than a symbolic gesture; its practical purpose was to enhance the efficiency of the Central Committee's control over the local party apparatus. Knowing the ineffectiveness of administrative means of control, Gierek decided to create a mechanism that functioned independently of the bureaucratic establishment and under his personal supervision. Afraid of being informed by deceitful advisers and thereby losing touch with events--as Gomulka did--Gierek made the press a channel linking him directly with society.

For every Communist regime, nationalism has served as an indispensable political engine to generate domestic support. Ideology is not a sufficient motivating force, especially in time of crisis, when the party must pretend to embody the best of the national tradition. It was no surprise, therefore, that

at the peak of the economic crisis, the government agreed, after
more than twenty years of hesitation, to restore the Royal
Castle in Warsaw. This symbol of statehood and past greatness
was destroyed at the beginning of the Second World War and no
Communist leader had had the courage to restore this reminder of
the period of the Polish-Lithuanian Commonwealth, Jagiellonian
Poland, and the struggle against Russian occupation. But then
the utility of ideology had dissipated, the castle had to be
rebuilt. In the official view, it is a "monument connecting
past, present and future generations of Poles (which) testifies
to the continuity of national achievements."(76)

The next major item on the agenda of nationalism was an
improvement of relations with the church. It had become an
unwritten custom in Poland that when a new "team" of Communists
gains control over the Central Committee they must first of all
present their credentials in Moscow. The second place to seek
an audience was with the Catholic prelate. (The United States
is third in the sequence when the Poles are looking for sympathy
and economic assistance.) The fact is that while the Catholics
and Communists in Poland are divided by their beliefs, they are
united in their nationalism, and both must coexist in a precar-
ious partnership. This explains the paradox of how it is
possible in Poland to be Communist and Catholic at the same
time.

The prelate, Cardinal Wyszynski, did not agree to receive
the Gierek team until the church had been granted title to
churches, monasteries and other ecclesiastical buildings located
in the former German territories. After that, the meeting
between the cardinal and Premier Jarosziewicz could be arranged,
with the prime minister pledging to improve relations with the
church. At this time, both sides found common interest in the
settlement of Polish-Vatican relations and the appointment of
Polish priests to head dioceses in Western Poland as full-
fledged bishops. Until 1972 they were formally apostolic
administrators. Ratification of the Polish-West German treaty
in 1972 induced the Vatican to recognize these territories as
Polish and reorganize their administrative structure to reflect
the pattern established in the Tenth Century.

Normalization of Poland's relations with the Vatican
encountered serious difficulties. The concordat of 1925 was
abrogated by the government as a gesture of protest against the
Vatican's appointment of German bishops to Polish dioceses
during the war. There were several such cases and not even the
Polish government-in-exile in London had been consulted by the
Vatican.

Relations were strained until, following the Soviet Unions'
reexamination of its policy toward the Vatican, Poland expressed
its willingness to "institutionalize" relations with the Holy
See. Olszowski had an audience with the pope, but only a
"permanent working relation" was established. The two sides
were divided over the status of the church in Poland. Supported
by the pope, the Polish Catholic hierarchy demanded constitutional recognition--a bill of rights for clergy and--
believers--while the government asked the church to "accept the

status quo . . . and recognize (Poland's) alliances, and
especially that with the Soviet Union."(77) This dispute is
still unresolved, but as a rule, church-state relations under
Gierek were better than at any time after the war.

As his predecessors did, Gierek used international issues
to promote domestic support for the system and for his leadership. Gierek attempted to take full advantage of detente to
enhance Poland's international prestige. He traveled abroad
frequently, visiting Washington and West European capitals while
Warsaw became a stopover for American presidents en route to
Moscow, a symbolic gesture intended to stress the special
relations between the United States and Poland and the value
attached to the quasi-independent role Poland had assumed in
East-West relations. As a special distinction, following
President Nixon's visit to Moscow in 1972, Poland was again
granted most-favored-nation status and thereby easy access to
American credits. The Russians, too, showed deference in trying
to allay one of Poland's greatest fears, another Soviet-Russian
deal behind Poland's back. Brezhnev's short visits to Warsaw on
his way to Bonn were intended to reassure the Poles and create a
feeling of consultation with the Soviets' junior allies. Gierek
was successful in creating an image as a respected European
leader, and hoped that impression would strengthen his leadership over Poland.

More important to Gierek than his political concerns was
his economic problem, which, of course, contained dramatic
political implications. Huge investments were required to
revitalize and modernize industry, and owing to a shortage of
capital, Gomulka had chosen to restrict consumption and have
unemployment at about half a million as a way of extracting the
fiscal means for expansion. "Savings" were to made in such
areas as construction of new apartments, development of light
industry and improvements in transportation, while prices on
food, fuel and some other basic commodities were allowed to
rise. On top of that, a system of economic incentives was
designed to increase productivity and reduce most wages. In
Gierek's time, the new international climate gave Poland a
chance to carry on an old pattern of simultaneous economic
relations with Russia and the West. Poland's rapid industrialization at the end of the Nineteenth Century was made possible
by Western capital and the easy availability of Russian markets.
Polish economists pointed out that now detente had opened up new
possibilities and that Poland, already highly industrialized and
in possession of a skilled labor force, should be able to
imitate the Japanese in making foreign trade a major source of
national wealth. Poland was richer in natural resources than
Japan and labor costs were lower; thus, what the country needed
was technological know-how and a certain amount of hard currency
to initiate production of exportable goods. Credits from
Western countries and accelerated expansion of foreign trade
were to provide Poland with investment finance.

TABLE II

Dynamics of Gross National Production
in Poland (1951-1979) (78)

| Year | Previous Year = 100 | 1950 = 100 |
|------|---------------------|------------|
| 1950 | 115.1 | 100.0 |
| 1951 | 107.5 | 107.5 |
| 1952 | 106.2 | 114.2 |
| 1953 | 110.5 | 126.1 |
| 1954 | 110.5 | 139.4 |
| 1955 | 108.4 | 151.1 |
| 1956 | 107.0 | 161.7 |
| 1957 | 110.7 | 179.1 |
| 1958 | 105.5 | 189.0 |
| 1959 | 105.2 | 198.8 |
| 1960 | 104.3 | 207.5 |
| 1961 | 108.2 | 224.4 |
| 1962 | 102.1 | 229.1 |
| 1963 | 106.9 | 265.0 |
| 1964 | 106.7 | 261.5 |
| 1965 | 107.0 | 279.8 |
| 1966 | 107.1 | 299.7 |
| 1967 | 105.7 | 316.8 |
| 1968 | 109.0 | 365.3 |
| 1969 | 102.9 | 355.3 |
| 1970 | 105.2 | 373.8 |
| 1971 | 108.1 | 404.1 |
| 1972 | 110.6 | 446.8 |
| 1973 | 110.8 | 495.1 |
| 1974 | 110.4 | 546.8 |
| 1975 | 109.0 | 595.9 |
| 1976 | 106.8 | 636.4 |
| 1977 | 105.0 | 668.2 |
| 1978 | 103.0 | 688.2 |
| 1979 | 97.9 | 672.4 |

Gierek continued the Gomulka policy of emphasizing techno-logical modernization and expansion of heavy industry, but he concluded that Poland could afford simultaneous growth of light industry without disrupting the economy. Huge investments were channeled into these two branches of industry, while the government attempted to counter inflation by importing consumer goods from the West, relying on domestic agricultural produc-tion, improving management and encouraging small private business.

For political reasons farm prices were not allowed to be set by free market forces. But Gierek did discontinue the system of forced deliveries of meat, milk and grain to the state at artificially low prices. This was an important concession to the farmers who had been chafing under such a forced-allocation system since the Nazi occupation. When the opportunity for

additional income presented itself, the peasants responded with
increased supplies, enabling the government to expand exports.

Modernized methods of management also contributed to a
higher rate of economic development under Gierek's leadership.
Although it was not described as a reform--so as not to raise
suspicions of revisionism or irritate the Soviets--some degree
of decentralization of administrative functions was allowed to
take place. This devolution was quite modest, however, and was
applied only to the most egregious cases. In the main, the
system of centralized planning was left intact.

Poland's expanded economic relations with the West were
offset by further integration of Poland's economy into the
Soviet bloc. Designed for this purpose were so-called common
enterprises, reminiscent of Stalin's joint stock companies. It
became common practice to finance industrial projects in the
Soviet Union with capital from one or more countries of the
bloc.(79) In Poland's case, there were numerous bilateral
agreements requiring Poland to make low-interest credits available to the Russians while Poland borrowed at much higher rates
from the West. In some cases Poland had to liquidate existing
plants and abandon new projects to avoid competition with Soviet
goods. The making of this pattern of cooperation a classic
example of societas leonina.

Soviet benefits were both political and economic. With the
capital of its client states, Russia was, of course, able to
strengthen its own economy. The Russians exported to bloc
countries low-quality manufactures in exchange for goods whose
production required investment of hard currency. The best known
example was the Polish export of ships, including tankers, to
the Soviet Union. Since Poland did not manufacture instruments
for navigation and lacked sufficient supplies of iron ore, it
had to purchase these items on West European markets, paying in
scarce dollars, only to deliver the ships to Russia for non-
convertible, or soft, rubles.

Poland's economic and political relations with two other
immediate neighbors, East Germany and Czechoslovakia, were on a
much more equal footing.

It was unrealistic to expect improvement in Polish-East
German relations as long as Gomulka and Walter Ulbricht remained
in power; their mutual distrust was too great.(80) Ulbricht
regarded Gomulka as a nationalist and a revisionist, while
Gomulka suspected that Ulbricht's willingness to send tanks to
Poland in 1956 was motivated by a hope that territorial changes
were still possible, particularly with respect to Szczecin.
Finally, Gomulka, like other Poles, never forgot Ulbricht's
statement describing Hitler's attack on Poland as the conquest
"of the gentry by German workers."(81)

Radical changes occurred when Erich Honecker and Edward
Gierek replaced the old rivals. Within a few years both governments and people were brought together as never before,
discovering a mutual interest in rapprochement.

However, an "open border" experiment, introduced at the end
of 1971 and enabling thirty million Poles and East Germans to
cross the border, caused concern on both sides. Besides many

unpleasant incidents, the uncontrolled tourism caused problems
in Poland's balance of payments because of the attractiveness of
the East German market for Polish consumers.(82)  From 1973 to
1980, when the East Germans closed the border following the
Solidarity ferment in Poland, fiscal means were employed to
control cross-border movements.

The first five years of Gierek's rule produced what looked
like an economic miracle.  The impressive growth of Poland's
gross national product encouraged the authorities to forecast
euphorically that by 1980 Poland would become a major industrial
power in Europe.  Due to steeply rising imports, however,
Poland's foreign debt grew from $1.2 billion in 1971 to $7.6
billion in 1975.  By 1980 it had reached 10 percent of GNP; $25
billion was owed to foreign banks and governments.  At the same
time, the Soviet Union substantially increased the price of the
oil it supplied Poland and a recession in Western Europe cut
demand for Polish imports.(83)

Gierek's reaction was characteristic.  The regime acted to
reduce domestic consumption of food as a means of sustaining
food exports to pay for foreign capital.  The political atmosphere deteriorated immediately but the explosion in 1976 was
caused by sudden and drastic price increases.  Overnight the
government raised the prices of basic commodities an average of
70 percent; the price of some goods was doubled.  Instan-
taneously, workers in several major enterprises went on strike
and the regime withdrew the price "corrections" the very same
day the increases were announced.

In retaliation, Gierek responded with a wave of repression,
which only served to increase popular disaffection.  In addition, the government expanded the so-called commercial sale of
basic commodities available at market prices (in some cases 200
percent above the subsidized price), overtly dividing the nation
into rich and poor.  Another byproduct of the chronic shortages
was a dramatic expansion of the black market.

Gierek and his team committed numerous economic errors.
Like his predecessors, of course, he neglected agriculture, and
private farmers in particular.  Polish peasants have been
haunted by a fear of collectivization and concerned by the lack
of a clear constitutional provision which would guarantee
private ownership of the land and put the issue to rest.  At the
same time, the regime provided huge subsidies to collectivized
agriculture, which accounted for about 30 percent of Poland's
farmland.  Inadequate assistance to the private sector coupled
with waste in the fiscally-favored socialized sector only served
to aggravate this vital problem.

The principal source of the disaster that brought Poland's
economy to the brink of ruin in 1980, however, was extravagant
borrowing from the West.  Foreign credits became a substitute
for fundamental structural reforms that were recommended as
early as 1956 but were rejected for fear the party would lose
control over the economy.

Precious foreign capital was used ineffectively.  The
centrally controlled economy lacked the flexibility to absorb
financial and technological resources and employ them produc-

tively so as to compete on Western markets. Large portions of the foreign credits were wasted on gigantic industrial projects like the Katowice Steelworks, built at a cost of $2 billion without, so far, providing a penny in return.

Finally, for several years the government had been using borrowed hard currency to supplement domestic consumption. When, in the summer of 1980, hard currency was not sufficient to supply domestic markets with food, Gierek, like Gomulka in December of 1970, moved to curtail domestic consumption by further expanding "commercial" sales at the expense of subsidized retail sales within the reach of ordinary people. This became the detonator for a national revolt, this time one that shook the foundations of the system, not only in Poland but throughout the bloc. Instead of the socialist democracy, self-government and socialist welfare that Gierek had promised, Poland found itself conquered by a coalition of its own Army and security forces. Thus Soviet-style socialism was transformed into a fascist-like political system based on penury and desperation.

## The State of War

So far, as in classical drama there are three acts to the 1980 crisis in Poland. During the first stage there appeared to be a search for a modus vivendi between Solidarity and the Communist state. Both sides viewed the revolt as a justified expression of public discontent over the political corruption and "economic voluntarism" of the Gierek era. The authorities followed a strategy of general retreat to avoid a head-on collision with the assertive union. But it was a policy of trading concessions for the time required to consolidate power, and when the party itself became infected with the virus of democracy and to a great extent disintegrated, the communist loyalists, entrenched behind the military--internal security forces, refused to negotiate further and instead launched a campaign to portray Solidarity as an organization manipulated by a small band of anti-patriotic, anti-socialist and anti-Soviet extremists. The imposition of martial law, the so-called "knock-out" solution by physical means, came to the accompaniment of an ultraorthodox interpretation of events by the authorities. Thus, Poland's economic, social and political troubles were ascribed to the evil machinations of the Western imperialists who aided counterrevolutionary elements in Poland. Poland's problems, it was proclaimed, were caused not by the pathology of socialism, but by not having a sufficient degree of socialism; a view which for years has been advanced by ideologically dogmatic elements in Soviet Russia and East Germany neighbors.

---

This section is included in my article, "Poland's Quo Vadis," published in Current History, November 1982.

Act I:  A Search for Partnership.  The political essence of
the 1980 revolt was that of restricting the monopolistic nature
of communism by introducing elements of limited government.  It
was undertaken with the help of a written social contract which
enumerated in detail the fundamental and particular rights and
obligations of each side.  This contract--the August 1980 Gdansk
Agreement--endorsed the key axioms of the Communist system,
including the principle of one-party rule which was secured by a
declaration that the Solidarity trade union would not transform
itself into a political organization.  It implied that Solidarity would confine its activities to bread-and-butter issues;
a very narrowly defined form of loyal opposition with no right
to ask for free elections.  Another clause guaranteed the
union's support for the "collective ownership of the means of
production--the essence of socialism in Poland," a recognition
of the leading role of the communist party and the existing
system of alliances.

Once the elementary principles of the Soviet system received formal endorsement, the authorities legalized the
existence of the "new, independent, self-governing labor
union...genuinely representing the working class."  The union
was entitled to "conduct collective bargaining" with the government, to exercise the "right to strike" with assurance of
"security for strikers and supporters."  This newly established
contractual relationship between the state and workers in Poland
guaranteed also the "freedom of the press, opinion, and publication," to be implemented by "access to the mass media," and,
extremely important in predominantly Roman Catholic Poland, the
freedom of religion.  Finally, in addition to a long list of
provisions having to do with working conditions and retirement,
the Agreement contained the general clause authorizing the union
to "pass public judgement on key decisions determining the
standard of living of the population, including the principles
governing the division of national income into consumption and
investment."(84)

The Gdansk Agreement was an attempt to reconcile two
conflicting models of politics, notably democracy, with the
power flowing from the bottom up, and communist autocracy, where
the prevailing current is from the top downward.  As a union
official noted, the "greatest success of Solidarity is that it
was formed and exists in a system of totalitarian power."(85)
Although the newly created union pledged not to undermine
socialism in Poland, this de facto political organization broke
the communist monopoly over the economy, information and ideology.  It acquired a veto power over almost every aspect of
Polish politics.  After thirty-five years of monopolistic
practices, the Communist Party found itself face-to-face with an
organized and legal opposition representing the workers.  For
the party it was certainly a political humiliation and a fearful
precedent.  The emergence of Solidarity put into question the
entire ideological foundation of the Soviet-like state.

During the first few months following the Gdansk Agreement,
there was a good deal of optimism regarding the attainment of a
modus operandi between the party and Solidarity.  As a matter of

fact, the party already had become accustomed to an openly competitive coexistence with the church, and an expansion of this dualism to a political triad could contribute to the stability of the system. While the party and the church shared only a sentiment of patriotism, Solidarity was not only patriotic, it appeared to accept the principles of socialism. Such a patriotic-socialistic platform was expected by some to guarantee an over-all political symmetry between the union and the party and to reduce the area of confrontation to other than the essential axioms of the system, respected but never endorsed by the church.

But the reality was quite different. Both organizations had grossly unequal resources at their command among the people. In the few months following its formation, Solidarity developed grassroots support of over ten million members. It became a dynamic union representing the entire Polish nation, and received the support of the church. The party, on the other hand, could claim no more than three million members, and a third of them were members of Solidarity. This was a dismal situation for the party, credited, to be sure, but not surprising, perhaps, for having led Poland into an "economic catastrophe unequaled in 200 years."(86) In addition, there was the problem that the party was widely regarded as a Trojan horse for Soviet hegemony in Poland. During the brief tour of Stanislaw Kania as party leader, after the fall of Gierek, there was a popular rhyme in Poland: "Better Kania than Vanya"-- Vanya, being a diminutive of the Russian name Ivan. As well as anything, this slogan expressed the Polish reasons for acceptance of Communist rule.

Other factors, as well, impeded the formation of a partnership between Solidarity and the party. The union had no faith in the sincerity of official support for the program of renewal, suspecting such support was a tactic intended to restore stability and allow for the reversal of the trend toward democratization. The party continued to be regarded as dishonest, opportunistic and unwilling to pay the price of coalition. The union concluded, therefore, that unless the links between the party and the institutions securing its domain were severed and the institutions were placed under public control, the communists would never stop searching for a restoration of the status quo ante August 1980. It is significant that the main areas of contention between Solidarity and the party involved control over economic enterprises, radio, television, the press, police and education--that is, control over the key pillars of the state. For the union, the Gdansk Agreement was just the first step toward renewal, for the party it was meant to be the end of the affair.

In its comprehensive and well prepared drive against the communist strongholds, Solidarity employed the potent weapons of strikes and demonstrations to force the authorities to retreat. The plausible threat of a nationwide general strike appeared the most effective political instrument directed against the state, since such action would paralyze the country and result in the union's takeover of the administrative functions of the state.

The consequence of a general strike would have revolutionary
implications, but despite several close calls, a general strike
was averted and some optimism continued to prevail. Both sides
appeared united by patriotic impulses: "Poles have come to an
agreement before and will reach one now," argued Lech Walesa.
"Without a compromise, we shall plunge into chaos and it may end
in fraternal violence. Who will take the responsibility for all
that?"(87)

However, negotiations were becoming less productive once a
gradual hardening of positions became evident. These difficulties were compounded by the growing influence of militants
within the union, once Solidarity became a kind of bandwagon for
every possible sort of opposition to the communist system,
including organizations like the Confederation of Independent
Poland (KNP) which favored free elections as a means to
terminate the communist system in the country. "The union was
not created to make compromises, but to smash the totalitarian
system in our country," one of the radicals declared.(88) At
the same time, the hard-liners in the regime, those who favored
a so-called "knock-out" or "power solution" emerged to organize
groups such as the Katowice Forum and the Poznan Forum.

The prospect of chaos created conditions for the authorities to recapture some of their lost legitimacy. When, in
March 1981, Solidarity called a strike alert as a prelude to a
general strike protesting police brutality in the eviction of
union members from a public building in Bydgoszcz, the Politburo
warned that the entire "country faces a serious danger" and that
"it is in the common interest of all Poles urgently to find a
way out of the situation."(89) This message implied that the
party had not relinquished its responsibility for Poland's
destiny and intended to challenge the union. For the time being
a showdown was avoided as national meetings of both Solidarity
and the party were scheduled.

Act II: Polarization. The second phase of the Polish
crisis began in July 1981, when the Ninth Extraordinary Congress
of the Polish United Workers Party met in Warsaw. The party
convened under strong pressure from its rank and file to remove
the stigma of corruption, incompetence and economic misman-
agement, to regroup its forces and make badly needed personnel
changes. To check the spread of Solidarity, the party clearly
had to refurbish its image and structure, and it was not
Marxism-Leninism and, in particular, democratic centralism that
the party delegates used as a guide, but a spirit of populism,
democracy and the accountability of party officials to their
constituencies.

By the conclusion of the Ninth (Extraordinary) Congress in
July 1981, an entirely new ideological composition of the party
had emerged, since for Communist Poland, the Ninth Congress was
the first opportunity to practice democracy within the party.
There was free discussion exposing fundamental political differences among party members, and a deep distrust for top party
bureaucrats. And there was secret balloting: The electoral
slogan of the radicals for a "crossing-out of the party
apparatus" helped produce a sharp reduction in the number of

apparatchiks on the Central Committee chosen by the Congress
delegates.

In comparing the composition of the Central Committees
elected by the Eighth and Ninth Congresses, one is struck by the
fact that the proportion of Communist party professionals fell
from over 50 percent in 1971 to about 8.5 percent while the
combined representation of workers, foremen, farmers and intellectuals roughly doubled from about 30 percent to more than 60
percent (31.5 percent workers and foremen, 13 percent intellectuals, 18.5 percent farmers(.(90)  Moreover, 20 percent of
the new Central Committee, or forty-one members, were also
members of Solidarity.  One of them was even elected to the
Politburo.

Of equal significance was the Communist confession that the
party is not a universal organization representing all of Polish
society.  Although this point has always been implicit in the
formal existence of a multiparty system, for a long time it was
assumed that all non-Communist political organizations would
eventually disband once the elementary stages of socialist
construction had been attained.  Two satellite political organizations, the United Peasant Group (ZSL) and the Democratic Group
(SD)--pledged total loyalty to the Communists and to Marxism-
Leninism and joined the Front of National Unity (FJN) under
Communist leadership.  This, in effect, deprived these quasi-
political parties of their own identity; Poland has correctly
been classified as a one-party state.

The necessity to restructure the FJN system was also
recognized.  It was in response to a search for political
identity by the non-Communist political organizations searching
for ways to disassociate themselves from the Communists' failures and to exploit the catastrophic decline of Communist power
by filling the vacuum.  Both the ZSL and the SD have developed
their own political platforms, focusing on economic and
political reforms with an emphasis on partnership instead of
subordination to the Communist Party.

It was proposed to change the FJN to the Front of National
Agreement, in reference to the pre-World War II practice of
nationwide political partnerships among a number of parties and
social organizations willing to work with the government.  This
new front was intended to become a self-governing instead of
Communist-dominated forum, drawing together all politically
articulate groups in Poland, including the Catholic Church and,
eventually, Solidarity.  Among the most urgent tasks was reform
of the electoral law and the possible return to a traditional
bicameral parliament and meaningful elections.(91)  It became
extremely awkward for the party to deny society the right to
free elections after the party had adopted such a practice
itself.

The party, too, has moved to broaden its constituency.
With its policies discredited, the party needed to acquire and
claim as its own the relative popularity of the Polish Army.
The party invited General Wojciech Jaruzelski, Commander of the
Army, to take the office of prime minister and the First Secre-
tary of the Communist Party.  From the ideological point of

view, it was even more discrediting to appoint a Catholic to the rank of Cabinet minister in Poland, but unlike the historical compromise in Italy, the Polish version demonstrates the weakness of the Communists and a sharp departure from the standards set by the Soviets for a "healthy" communist state.

But the party Congress failed to institutionalize pluralism in Poland. As one observer noted:

> the delegates appeared preoccupied with settling old scores, apportioning blame for the crisis and voting out of office anyone tainted by the mistakes of the previous leadership. Remarkably little attention was paid to the future and the meeting failed to agree on a vision and a program for getting out of the crisis. (92)

For the party to lead the country out of the crisis it was desirable for it to take some distance from the daily administration of the country with all the freedom and enlarged perspective that would afford, but it didn't. Instead, it chose to remain red tape of the system, identified with every shortcoming that entailed, and despite changes in leadership and internal discipline the party bureaucracy survived the Congress with its personnel and prerogatives largely intact. The party was afraid to relinquish its claim to a monopoly of power for fear that would be equivalent to abdication from power. The party did nothing to create the conditions for a partnership with those political forces eager both to accept socialism and to respect the party's unique position as arbiter of the system and its sole voice in national security affairs. The party had not formally reformed the Leninist-Stalinist concept of its leading role. So the democratization within the party was not allowed to be felt through a democratization of the country: such a coalition government representing the Polish triad of the communist party, the union and the church.

Specifically, the Congress failed to introduce a system of "contractual" democracy, which on the one hand would guarantee a genuine political pluralism in Poland, and, on the other hand, preclude the possibility of struggle for political survival. To achieve this result, a meaningful share of power would have to be apportioned to several political parties, including the communists, and the participants allowed to engage in a political dialogue, but precluded from eliminating each other by such means as "knocking" or voting each other out.(93)

Under the circumstances, the democratization of the party had been a mistake. More decentralized structure weakened the ability of the central authorities to solve the pressing national problems or effectively to counterbalance Solidarity. And while it produced a diffusion of rank and file members who were no longer bound together by strict enforcement of party discipline it also resulted in the strengthening of the hierarchically organized bureaucratic core of the party. These professional party cadres, with the greatest stake in the system, quickly formed an alliance with the internal security forces and the top political echelon of the Army: a core of the communist system composed. Without a program of national democratization, the apparatus of coercion became the party's sole source of power.

In the eyes of the general public, the initiation of democratic reforms limited to the party alone was just another maneuver designed to stabilize the regime, a new way to manipulate Polish society. It also was seen as a convenient method of removing Gierek's Silesian gang from power and of covering over instead of revising the centralistic-bureaucratic and monopolistic propensities of communism.

Soon after the Congress adjourned, communist dogmatism resurfaced with the party's rejection of a grand coalition; an unrealistic attempt, it was said, to reconcile forces representing dialectically antagonistic classes. Solidarity was portrayed as a counterrevolutionary organization and the idea of socialist pluralism was dismissed as a politically naive expectation that two parallel authorities could function in the same state. This new orthodoxy marked a change in attitude toward dialogue with Solidarity, previously regarded as the only feasible way of dealing with the crisis.

By the autumn of 1981, the authorities were prepared to employ "any means which may be required," according to Stefan Olszowski, a prominent conservative member of the Politburo. This was meant to say that the party was no longer bound by its self-imposed restrictions on the use of force. Instead of encouraging the union to negotiate, the authorities issued a list of demands, a form of ultimatum that Solidarity cease to act as a political party, end its criticisms of the government, desist from all strikes and abandon all international activities.(94) It is thus evident that the reform Congress had the paradoxical outcome of strengthening the opponents of reform of tilting the center of power in the direction of the internal security apparatus and, owing to the visible disintegration of the party, creating a false impression of a power vacuum--an invitation to the union to take politically decisive steps.

The emergence of a free, independent, self-governing trade union in Poland marked a reversal in such a system of the obligatory flow of power from the top downward; in doing so it emulated an important characteristic familiar to democratic societies. Not surprisingly, considerable ambiguity surrounded the political status of Solidarity. It was neither a trade union nor a political party; rather, it was a spontaneous, socio-political mass movement involving about 70 percent of the Polish labor force. The leading Polish dissident Adam Michnik explains:

> Solidarity has, in a sense, been everything: a labor
> union organization in the factory; the recognized
> prosecutor of criminals hidden in the citadel of
> power; the defender of political prisoners, of legal-
> ity, of independent culture--everything, in fact,
> except one thing. It is not, and did not wish to be,
> a political party. It has not struggled to gain

power. Those who laid that charge against it has done
so in bad faith.
Solidarity has become a multifunctional social movement that has played the role of guarantor of the
nascent Polish democracy and has been at the same time
its fundamental component.(95)

In contrast to the party congress, Solidarity celebrated
its first anniversary by debating concrete measures for resolving the national crisis. There could be no doubt that the
union already had transformed itself into a political organization with a broad national constituency. It was ready to
focus on a political platform, which, among other recommen-
dations, favored cuts in military spending, comprehensive fiscal
reform, decentralization of the economy by giving workers a
voice in running factories and the establishment of an
independent judiciary. One observer noted that "it is like a
new constitution approved by the genuine representatives of the
ten million members of the union."(96)
The Solidarity Congress established what was in effect a
second Polish government based in Gdansk. The question of free
elections, which without a doubt would sweep the communist party
from power, received extensive consideration, but the demand was
eventually dropped in favor of direct negotiations with the
authorities. The union, however, did not hesitate to challenge
Soviet supremacy in Eastern Europe. In a provocative act of
defiance the congress called on "working class people" throughout the bloc to establish independent self-governing unions like
Solidarity. As noted by Trybuna Ludu, the Polish party
newspaper, this appeal "set Solidarity against the socialist
world."(97) TASS, meantime, declared that from Moscow's point
of view it was a "call ·for struggle against the socialist
system, openly provocative and impudent toward the socialist
countries."(98) Indeed, solidarity appeared ready to shake the
foundations of the Soviet empire in Europe calling for a Spring
of Nation against the Soviet domination.
Although the union had not renounced its vow to respect the
leading role of the Communist Party--that is, it did not openly
endorse free national elections--it clearly was no longer a
"loyal opposition" faithful to the principles of socialism. It
declared itself to be an independent and dominant political
force in the nation, and some of its members inclined to
negotiate with the regime denounced as collaborators.(99) This
meant that socialism was no longer a point of common ground
between the union and the party. Rejection of socialism was
viewed as contrary to the national interest of a Polish nation
now left unprotected against "fraternal aid" from Moscow. The
rules of the game were changed, and the authorities felt free to
solve the crisis, as Olszowski had said, by "any means."
The congress also exposed two essential weaknesses of
Solidarity as a political party. First of all, its ideological
diversity became apparent. As long as it was concerned with the
economic issues of the traditional trade union, Solidarity
appeared united by a common cause. As a political organization

it was divided along three lines of orientation: social democratic, Christian democratic and a grouping of anti-Communists
(liberals). This ideological heterogeneity prevented the
congress from centralizing authority in the National Committee.
The union clearly outnumbered its rival, but Solidarity never
became a well-tuned political instrument capable of matching the
numerically inferior but organizationally superior communist
party.

Secondly, political particularism played a damaging role.
The union had been wasting its resources on relatively minor
issues of local concern, causing the strike weapon to depre-
ciate. This was an ominous development which eventually
prompted Solidarity to escalate its conflict with the party by
reaching for free elections as a more effective weapon. But,
for the time being, the union agreed to withhold its demand for
free elections. It gave the party a two-month period of grace
to reach a political compromise that would have meant the end of
the party's power monopoly. The party was not only unwilling to
abdicate, it was unable to act at all. A political stalemate
resulted that had to be overcome by a third force. The essential question was whether this third force would be foreign or
domestic.

Act III: Knock-Out--The Lesser Evil. Poland's options by
the end of 1981 were few indeed.(100) Hypothetically, the
apparatus of the Communist Party could still prevail over a
fragmented Solidarity. This "return to order," advocated by the
most dogmatic elements of the party hierarchy, would spell the
end of the idea of even the most moderate economic reforms
approved during the brief period of renewal. In fact, the
entire program of renewal would be put back in deep freeze since
political control of every aspect of economic and social life
would have to have priority over economic efficiency. In
historical perspective, it would set conditions for another
round of Poland's vicious circle with the possibility of violence on a national scale.

A second contingency, that of free elections with a land-
slide victory for Solidarity, was likely to produce general
chaos. The union was a spontaneous and euphoric movement unable
to preserve its internal cohesiveness. Its centrifugal forces,
so difficult to contain even under conditions of Soviet pressure, would scatter Solidarity into a great number of rival
parties; the union had neither a comprehensive ideology, an
institutional framework, nor the political expertise required to
exercise power in a coherent fashion. The union, to be sure,
had proved effective in "washing out" communism in Poland; it
became a formidable challenge to the oligarchic system, but it
never demonstrated the kind of maturity necessary to assume all
the functions of the state in the Soviet dominated Eastern
Europe. An opposition it could help to democratize politics in
Poland. Yet, alone, it could not assure a stable democracy.

Moreover, it is necessary to recognize the certainty of
Soviet intervention before free elections could be organized.
As in 1945, when the Yalta Agreement provided for "free and
unfettered" Polish elections, such an eventuality today is no

less a luxury beyond the reach of the Poles. The Soviets
tolerated what they considered numerous insults from the union
and they showed readiness to allow compromise on several sacred
canons of Marxism-Leninism. But at this point they would not
accept a rollback of the Soviet system in Eastern Europe, nor
could they tolerate instability that threatened Soviet security
on the Western frontiers of their emporium. Any "fraternal aid"
rendered to Poland would be bloody, expensive and prolonged.
Yet, in the Soviet view, that would be preferable to the consequences of free elections in Poland which would alter the
balance of power in Europe. For Poland, the final outcome of a
Soviet-led invasion could de facto reduce Poland to the status
of a Soviet republic, with the possibility of East Germans
assuming "temporary" administration justified by economic
concerns over a portion of the Oder-Neisse territories. Having
decided to take such a drastic step as to invade Poland, and
having no trust in the native communists, Moscow, already
discredited in world opinion, could be inclined to solve the
Polish problem once and for all (as it tried after the 1863
uprising or following the Soviet-Nazi Pact in 1939). Armed
Soviet intervention in Poland would constitute a threat not only
to Poland's national independence but to its national identity.

The Roman Catholic Church is the only institution not
associated with the communist system that appears equipped to
take over functions of the state. However, despite the encouragement it received from Solidarity, the church consistently
rejected excessive involvement in politics. The church's
mission like the role assumed by the Russian Orthodox Church
during two centuries of the Mongol occupation, is to protect the
Polish nation by preserving its culture and its values. In that
respect, the church has proved very successful, whose political
ambitions in the past have been channeled into a concern for
issues related to freedom of conscience, social justice and
national traditions. The church has tremendous authority in
Poland stemming from its superb leadership and a millenium of
political experience. Since World War II, the church's
political strategy has been to oppose the policies of communism
while avoiding destabilization of the system for fear of Soviet
invasion. Regardless of their ideological antagonism, the
church and the communist party have depended on each other for
survival. The church has helped the party maintain a consensus
based on an understanding that there is no realistic alternative
to Communist rule, while the party protects the Polish nation,
including the church, from the Russians. The communist party,
therefore, has two masters; one is in the Kremlin, the other is
the Primate of Poland.

Although dogmatic and unbending on moral issues, the church
in Poland has demonstrated a remarkable degree of political
flexibility. In its relations with Communist authorities, it
has been guided by national interests even if that required
doctrinal compromise or even occasional disobedience of the
Vatican, as in the case of the Oder-Neisse Line. Religious
practice in Poland is a political act, a manifestation of
possible resistance to the state and its ideology. The church

is viewed popularly as a martyr to communist oppression, a symbol of hope and the curator of a national identity threatened by communism.

In its political duel with communism, the church has employed the policy invented by the party, the strategy of juxtaposing the state against the Roman Catholic hierarchy, but the sharp edge has been turned against the state in the invidious comparison between the 7 percent of Poles who are communists and the 90 percent who are Catholics. For all its popularity, the church was no more able than any other domestic force to shield Poland from Soviet domination, but it does possess the capacity to minimize its historical impact. The greatest achievement of the church in post-war Poland has until now been to preserve ideological pluralism despite the communist monopoly of power.

Several attempts to check the authority of the church have failed. Neither sponsorship of splinter groups such as National Catholics, nor attempts to separate Catholic intellectuals from workers and peasants, nor harassment nor loud campaigns accusing the church of wanting to give away the western parts of Poland to the Germans have ever succeeded. The effect of these efforts has been not to discredit the church, but to discredit the party. In the triangular pattern of Polish pluralism, the church has assumed the role of arbiter of the national interest and mediator of last resort between the unions and the party. Although patronizing the unions, the church would commit its prestige on the party's behalf were the national sovereignty in jeopardy. It amounts to the leading role of the church in Poland and it is a painful lesson for the party, which is still unable to separate overall domination from governing and administration.

The source of the church's tremendous political authority is its apolitical appearance and an emphasis on human rights, including the right "to confess Christ in public." The church, according to the late Stefan Cardinal Wyszynski, has "not only the right but the moral and religious duty to defend the faith, our traditions, and our Polish culture."(101) For this reason, during the recent crisis, the church preferred to keep its distance from politics, acting only as a mediator between Solidarity and the party. To perform its historical duties, the church cannot afford to risk the consequences of direct political involvement, and the wisdom of this approach has been vindicated many times. In 1,000 years of Christianity in Poland, the church has survived intact and continues to speak freely, even after the imposition of martial law.

This situation left the Army reinforced by the internal security units as the sole institution in Poland capable to respond to the crisis. Proclaiming to act in the interest of "national security and political stability," General Wojciech Jaruzelski, the commander-in-chief, premier and first secretary of the PUWP, imposed martial law.(102) The alleged purpose was to prevent violent confrontations between the party and Solidarity, to avoid civil war that assuredly would have brought in the Soviets. Thus the state of emergency and military rule have

been portrayed as a lesser evil to the consequences of free
elections.

The military is not a neutral force. It has a definite
pro-Soviet bias justified by the patriotic necessity of survival
in the Soviet dominated Eastern Europe. The military "knock-
out" was not an even-handed reaction against the Communist
bureaucracy and "extremists" within the union. The blows fell
almost exclusively on the latter. Under the pretext of removing
a group of "madmen" from Solidarity, the military destroyed the
entire union--the only genuinely representative body Poland had.
In the words of a Communist activist, the party was suddenly
left again without "competition," and the entire political stage
is now ours."(103) In effect, martial law eliminated Polish
society as a partner to decision-making and turned back the
clock to the days when political decisions were a function of
struggles among the competing group of a closed system, in the
present case, between the dogmatic and moderate wings of the
party.

The military regime in Poland may not be aware of how
superficial is its control of the Polish nation. As dismissed
editor of Gazeta Krakowska noted succinctly:

> Paradoxically, the people who hold power, it's gone
> to their heads that it was so easy to introduce
> martial law. Because of this they think it will be
> easy to rule. They begin to live in a world of
> fiction--there's a fascination with the technical
> aspects of it all, an illusion of power.
> The situation is just the opposite of what it was
> before martial law. Then there was a kind of euphoria
> in Solidarity. Power was just lying there in the
> street waiting to be picked up. So the situation is
> paradoxically reversed. The authorities are now
> living with the illusion that they are exercising
> power, and the society is living with its new real-
> ism.(104)

The final outcome of the struggle between the moderates and
the dogmatists is not yet known, but at this moment there is a
stalemate tilted to the dogmatic side. A prolonged suspension
of civil rights, political "verifications" (a practice common
under Stalinism), purges, calls for ideological purity, together
with an emphasis on work discipline rather than self-government
and decentralization, greatly outweigh the sporadic promises to
resume a dialogue and eventually introduce pluralism in Poland.
One must conclude, therefore, that the process of "socialist
renewal" under military supervision in Poland has a closer
resemblance to post-1968 "normalization" in Czechoslovakia than
it does to the prelude of democratization. The only unknown is
how patient Polish society is going to be, especially in view of
the fact that while martial law has produced temporary political

stability it has done very little to encourage economic stability or a solution to the structural problems of the Polish economy; that is, neither political nor economic sources of the recurrent Polish crisis have received attention, and economic decline continues.

Notes

1. Podstawy Nauk Politicznych, Dokumenty i Materialy, vol.
   I, 2nd edition (Warszawa: Ksiazka i Wiedza, 1972), pp.
   236-45.

2. Bronislaw Kusmierz, Stalin and the Poles (London: Hollis
   & Carter, 1949), pp. 218-221. Jan M. Ciechanowski,
   Powstanie Warszwskie (Londyn: Odnowa, 1971), pp. 221-48.
   Also, Karol Grunberg, Historia Polski w Latach 1939-1947
   Torun, 1971), p. 115.

3. Stefan Litauer, Zmierzch "Londynu" (Warszawa, Lodz:
   Spoldzielnia Wydawnicza "Czytelnik," 1945), p. 41.

4. J. K. Zawodny, Nothing But Honour (Stanford: Hoover
   Institution Press, 1978), Chapter 4.

5. Documents on Polish-Soviet Relations, 1939-1945, London
   Instytut Historyczny Imienia Generala Sikorskiego (ed.),
   (London: Haynemann, 1961-1967), vol. II, p. 578.
   Hereafter cited as DPSR.

6. DPSR, vol. II, p. 618.

7. Jozef Winiewicz, "Poland and the German Problem," Poland
   Today, January 1948, p. 3.

8. Stanislaw Mikolajczyk, The Rape of Poland (New York:
   McGraw-Hill Book Company, Inc., 1948), pp. 145-7.

9. Jan Borkowski, "Pertraktacje Przedwyborcze Miedzy Polska
   Partia Robotnicza i Polska Partia Socialistyczna a
   Polskim Stronnictwem Ludowym," Kwartalnik Historyczny,
   1964, No. 2.

10. Mikolajczyk, op. cit., p. 161.

11. The Polish Election, 19th January, 1947 (London: British
    Joint Committee for Polish Affairs, 1947), pp. 31-33.
    See also, Jozef Swiatlo, Za Kulisami Bezpieki i Partii
    (No publisher, 1954), p. 39.

12. The New York Times, January 19, 1947.

13. Samuel L. Sharp, Poland. White Eagle on a Red Field
    (Cambridge, Mass.: Harvard University Press, 1953), p.
    200.

14. An article signed by R, "The Fate of Polish Socialism,"
    Foreign Affairs, No. 1, October 1949, pp. 125ff.

15. Kurt L. London, "Eastern Europe in the Communist World,"
    in Robert F. Byrnes (ed.), The United States and Eastern

_Europe_ (Englewood Cliffs, N.J.: Prentice-Hall, Inc., 1967), p. 107.

16. Oskar Lange, _Dwie Drogi Rozwoju w Gospodace Swiatowej_ (Warsaw: Panstwowy Instytut Spraw Miedzynaradowych, 1950), p. 3. See also, Ignacy Rzendowski, "Handel Zagraniczny USA a Plan Marshala," _Nowe Drogi_, No. 9 (1948), pp. 226-245.

17. Jan F. Triska (ed.), _Constitution of the Communist Party States_, (Stanford, California: The Hoover Institution on War, Revolution and Peace, Stanford University, 1968), p. 333.

18. Quoted in _The New York Times_, April 16, 1948.

19. _The New York Times_, May 27, 1948.

20. Translation of the entire document can be found in Hansjakob Stehle, _The Independent Satellite_ (London: Fredrick A. Praeger, 1965), p. 306.

21. _The New York Times_, November 30, 1956.

22. _The New York Times_, March 12, 1957.

23. Vaclav L. Benes and Norman G. J. Pounds, _Poland_ (London: Ernest Benn Limited, 1970), p. 369.

24. _Concise Statistical Year Book of the Polish People's Republic_ (Warsaw: Published by Central Statistical Office), for 1966, pp. 43, 61; 1972, pp. 67, 87, 149.

25. Adam Bromke, _Poland's Politics: Idealism vs. Realism_ (Cambridge, Mass.: Harvard University Press, 1967, p. 135.

26. _The New York Times_, June 25, 1957.

27. Richard F. Staar, _Poland 1944-1962. The Sovietization of a Captive People_ (New Orleans: Louisiana State University Press, 1962), p. 94.

28. _The New York Times_, January 1, 1958.

29. _The New York Times_, February 15, 1959.

30. Bromke, _op. cit._, p. 136.

31. _The New York Times_, February 12, 1961.

32. _The New York Times_, July 27, 1960.

33. _The New York Times_, February 12, 1961.

126

34. The New York Times, September 14, 1961.

35. The New York Times, June 9, 1962.

36. The New York Times, June 7, 1962.

37. Jerzy Ptakowski, "The Fifth Polish Party Congress," East Europe, No. 1 (1969), p. 4.

38. Michael Gamarnikow, "Poland's Economic Recession," East Europe, No. 3 (1963), pp. 13ff.

39. Elizabeth K. Valkener, "The Catholic Church in Poland, 1945-1955", Review of Politics, No. 3 (1956), p. 306.

40. Trybuna Ludu, December 8, 1956.

41. Staar, op. cit., p. 255.

42. For more details see Alexander Bregman, "Gomulka's Long Hot Spring," East Europe, No. 8 (1966), pp. 2-14.

43. Michalina Vaughan, "A Multidimensional Approach to Contemporary Polish Stratification," Survey, No. 1 (1974), pp. 62ff.
    Also, Jan Szczepanski, "The Polish Intelligentsia. Past and Present," in Tadeusz N. Cieplak (ed.), Poland Since 1956 (New York: Twayne Publishers, Inc., 1972), pp. 104ff.

44. Leszek Kolakowski, "Permanent and Transitory Aspects of Marxism," in Pawel Mayewski (ed.), The Broken Mirror (New York: Random House, 1958), pp. 161-173.

45. Bromke, op. cit., p. 134.

46. Ryszard Turski and Eligiusz Lasota, "Polski Pazdziernik," Po Prostu, October 28, 1956.

47. Henryk Skolomowski, "Leszek Kolakowski--Fenomen Polskiego Marksizmu," Kultura, No. 5 (1969), p. 25.

48. Adam Bromke, "The 'Znak' Group in Poland," East Europe, No. 2 (1962), p. 11.

49. Gaston De Cerezy, "Gomulka and the Intellectuals," East Europe, No. 12 (1964), pp. 22ff.

50. "Freedom Manifesto of 34 Polish Intellectuals," in Cieplak (ed.), op. cit., p. 130.

51. Wiktor Troscianko, "Polish Journalism and the Censor," East Europe, No. 11 (1965), p. 13.

52. Wladislaw Gomulka, "Writers and Socialism," in Cieplak (ed.), op. cit., p. 138.

53. Zygmund Bauman, "Twenty Years After: The Crisis of Soviet-Type System," Problems of Communism, Nos. 11-12 (1971), p. 48.

54. "Nauki Wydarzen," Kultura, Nos. 6-7 (1968), pp. 77-8.

55. "Speech by Wladislaw Gomulka," Polish Perspectives, No. 4 (1968), p. xiii.

56. Kacek Kurun and Karol Modzelewski, "An Open Letter to the Party," in Julius Jacobson (ed.), Soviet Communism and the Socialist Vision (New Brunswick, N.J.: Transaction Books, 1972), p. 262.

57. Jan Nowak, "Conflict of Generations in Poland," East Europe, No. 5 (1968), p. 14.

58. "Resolution of the Union of Polish Writers, The City of Warsaw Branch," in Cieplak (ed.), op. cit., p. 148.

59. Jerzy Ptakowski, "Gomulka and His Party," East Europe, No. 5 (1967), p. 3.

60. Jerzy Ptakowski, "The Fifth Polish Party Congress," East Europe, No. 1 (1969), p. 4.

61. Ptakowski, "Gomulka and His Party," op. cit., p. 4.

62. The New York Times, July 1, 1965.

63. Jan Nowak, "The Struggle for Party Control," East Europe, No. 5 (1968), p. 4. And, Zygmund Bauman, "O Frustracji i o Kuglarzach," Kultura, No. 12/255 (1968), pp. 15-16.

64. Quoted in Ptakowski, "The Fifth Polish Party Congress," op. cit., p. 4.

65. Stanislaw Kozinski, "Consumption and the Market," Polish Perspectives, No. 3 (1968), pp. 28-9.

66. Jan Glowczyk and Marek Misiak, "The Future of the Economy," Polish Perspectives, No. 10 (1968), p. 13.

67. Michael Gamarnikow, "Another Step Toward Private Enterprise," East Europe, No. 1 (1968), p. 4.

68. Milovan Dzilas, "Wnioski z Polskiego Grudnia," Kultura, No. 3/282 (1971), p. 53.

128

69. Edward Gierek, "Przemowienie na VIII Plenum KC PZPR," (February 7, 1971), in Stanislaw Machete (ed.), Podstawy Nauk Politycznych, vol. I (Warszawa: Ksiazka i Wiedza, 1972), p. 408.

70. Trybuna Ludu, June 28, 1975.

71. Jan Nowak, "W Poszukiwaniu Trzeciej Drogi," Na Antenie, No. 95 (1971), p. 7.

72. Na Antenie, No. 112/113 (1972), p. 46.

73. "Rewolucja Palacowa," Na Antenie, No. 95 (1971), pp. 10 and 30.

74. Na Antenie, No. 127 (1973), p. 5.

75. February 19, 1971.

76. Trybuna Ludu, January 31, 1971.

77. The New York Times, June 29, 1972; and The Christian Science Monitor, November 28, 1973 and January 3, 1975.

78. Rocznik Statystyczny 1980 (Warszawa: Glowny Urzad Statystyczny, 1980), p. xxxii.

79. Stanislaw Gora and Zygmunt Krzyziak, Miedzynarodowa Spejializacja Produkcji Krajow RWPG (Warsaw: Panstwowe Wydawnictwo Gospodarcze, 1974), pp. 64-75. Also Jerzy Pekalski, "Struktura Obrotow Polsko-- Radzieckich," Zycie Gospodarcze, January 26, 1975, p. 13.

80. Erwin Weit, At the Red Summit (New York: Macmillan Publishing Co. Inc., 1973), p. 40.

81. George J. Fleming, "The Polish Eagle Looks West," East Europe, No. 10 (1967), p. 16.

82. The New York Times, June 24, 1973.

83. Janusz Rakowski, "Dlugi PRL po Zamachu," Kultura, No. 1 (1982), p. 129.

84. William F. Robinson (ed.), August 1980. The Strikes in Poland, Radio Free Europe Research, Munich, West Germany, October 1980, pp. 423-433.

85. Quoted in Newsweek, September 4, 1981, p. 53.

86. Edward Lipinski, a distinguished and senior economist, co-founder of KOR, quoted in John Darnton, "Polish Dissidents Disband Key Group," The New York Times, September 29, 1981.

87. Quoted in John Darnton, "Under Strike Threat, Labor Talks Begin in Warsaw," The New York Times, March 26, 1981.

88. Quoted in The New York Times, September 28, 1981.

89. Quoted in John Darnton, "Polish Regime Ends Party With Union Without Agreement," The New York Times, March 23, 1981.

90. Radio Free Europe Research, RAD Background Report/221 (Poland), August 3, 1981, p. 5.

91. Witold Jankowski, "'FJN' Sta sie Instytucja Czysto Formalna" (FJN Became a Purely Formal Institution), Sowo Powszechne, August 4, 1981.

92. Michael Dobbs, "Political Earthquake," The Washington Post, July 23, 1981.

93. Ryszard Skwarski, "Linia Podzialu. Linia Porozumienia" (Line of Division. Line of Agreement), Kierunki, October 8, 1981.

94. Trybuna Ludu, August 8-9, 1981.

95. Quoted in Radio Free Europe Research, RAD Background Report/260 (Poland), September 9, 1981, p. 3.

96. Quoted in The New York Times, October 8, 1981.

97. Quoted in John Darnton, "Polish Party Criticizes Union's Appeal," The New York Times, September 10, 1981.

98. Quoted in Dusko Doder, "Moscow Says Union Stages Open Fight," The Washington Post, September 11, 1981.

99. Andrzej Krzysztof Wroblewski, "I Zjazd Solidarnosci" (1st Congress of Solidarity), Polityka, October 4, 1981.

100. Lecture by Jerzy Wiatr, Gazeta Krakowska, December 10, 1981.

101. Quoted in Jan Nowak, "The Church in Poland," Problems of Communism, January-February, 1982, p. 15.

102. Trybuna Robotnicza, December 14, 1981. For more comments on martial law in Poland see J. B. De Weydenthal, "Poland's Parliament Ratifies the State of Emergency." Radio Free Europe, RAD Background Report/24, January 29, 1982, p. 4.

130

103. "Jak Partia Odzyskkuje Sily" (How the Party is Recovering Strength), _Trybuna Ludu_, January 16-17, 1982.

104. Quoted in John Darnton, "A Peek at Polish Campus Life: Defiant but Subdued," _The New York Times_, March 12, 1982.

# 4
# Post Scriptum

This most recent revolt in Poland is the fourth consecutive case of the use of force and deception against the Polish nation on behalf of the Communist status quo. If the vicious circle continues, the next revolt might escalate to the level of a violent national uprising, since all peaceful means to institutionalize even limited pluralism may have been exhausted. The Soviet-like system is inherently unable to overcome its monistic propensities regardless of the price extracted from the society. Jaruzelski's neo-Stalinism averted Soviet invasion, but only at the cost of dashing the hopes that liberalization and a higher standard of living might eventually materialize.

The main irony of the Polish situation is that the military rule in Poland halted evolution into a model originally recommended by the Big Three in Yalta. In a political sense, the post-World War II Poland was not patterned on now irrelevant Piast Poland, but on the Kingdom of Poland alternative set up in 1815 by the Congress of Vienna. This time enlarged to include the Oder-Neisse territories with a wide access to the Baltic Sea, the Polish state was again designed as a semi-independent buffer protecting Russia from military and ideological threat from the West. For this reason, the westward expansion of Poland was convenient for a Soviet Russia interested in weakening Germany and directing Poland against the West. It was also a compensation for territorial losses at the expense of the U.S.S.R. Poland, placed within comfortable borders and enjoying considerable autonomy guaranteed by her internationally recognized right to "free and unfettered" elections, was to be free of anxiety.

The elections were not intended to be a method to eliminate the influence of the Communists, but as an orderly installation of a legitimate "Russian party" in Poland. They were to assume a lasting political role as an umpire of the country's foreign policy and an important factor in domestic affairs. Regardless of their microscopic popularity, the Communists were entitled to enter the governing coalition, sharing power with indigenous parties such as peasants and socialists. This represented a

131

workable solution, a practical compromise between the Soviet search for security and Poland's ambition to be independent.

A critical importance was placed on the traditional Polish pursuit of self-determination. As a buffer state, Poland had to be politically stable and economically prosperous, a balancing factor in European politics capable of pacifying Russia's fear of the West, but friendly, not threatening, toward the West. Poland was to live according to her own values with an understanding that in foreign policy matters, Soviet interest must be assured priority. It was the flagrant Soviet violation of the spirit and letter of the Yalta Agreement, orchestrated by Moscow Communist monopolization of power, which in effect transformed the country into a notorious source of irritation in Europe.

This vision in Yalta of a Polish model of peaceful coexistence between a small nation and Soviet Russia should not be confused with Finish or Austrian neutrality. Poland had to be a pro-Soviet state, not a neutral or semi-neutral country, but permanently bound to Moscow by common foreign policy and development along the general principles of socialism. However, liquidation of institutional pluralism in Poland turned the country into a "sick man in Europe," and triggered enduring conflict between the Polish nation and its Communist rulers fruitlessly trying to find a substitute for a genuine pluralism and close ties with the West.

First, it was a mobilization to reconstruct the nation's economy. Cautious nationalism and restricted liberalism were added in the post-1956 period, and following the crisis of 1970, the Poles were to enjoy consumerism. All these measures were short lived and judged insufficient to buy lasting consensus. Liberal policies were never institutionalized, nationalism was manipulated to suit the Communists, and premature consumerism produced economic catastrophe. Once the regime ran out of gestures preserving the facade of democracy, it had to reach for methods which marked a return to practices typical at the time of takeover in the late 1940s.

The counterproductive Soviet determination that Poland should be a replica of the Soviet state has consequences far beyond the daily frustration of the Polish people. Stalin had wasted a unique historical opportunity to achieve a real Polish-Russian reconciliation. The barbarian policies of Nazi occupation had overshadowed Soviet crimes like the murder of Polish officers in Katyn, territorial changes, Soviet-Nazi collaboration in 1939 and during the Warsaw Uprising in 1944. Sovietization of Poland fueled anti-Russian feelings despite Soviet liberation from the Nazis and the four decades since World War II witnessed a gradual improvement of Poland's relations with West Germany. This is neither friendship nor admiration, but an acceptance and understanding demonstrated by a voluntary West German recognition of the Oder-Neisse line, and generous humanitarian aid to ease food shortages in Poland. Under the prudent leadership of the Roman Catholic church, the Poles have resisted the principal thrust of Sovietization moving closer to the western political and cultural ideas.

Thus, despite the similarity of Polish and Soviet security objectives vis-a-vis Germany, Poland is the least reliable member of the Warsaw Pact. The Soviets face hostile population on their western border, and communist Poland has been draining the economic and military resources of Soviet Russia.

The dismal condition of Poland is also a testimony to a failure of the Soviet system in general. It may be that nothing can be more embarrassing to the utopian self-image of a Communist society than recurring revolts of the workers by the workers against the "workers' state." Polish experience has epitomized all key pathological features of Russian communism: its oppressiveness, inequality, inefficiency, and Russian hegemonism. The reactionary nature of the Soviet system is also evident in its presentation of a genuine solidarity of the entire working class as a conspiratorial counter-revolutionary movement supported by Western imperialism.

Fear and defiance of Soviet Russia are the very essence of contemporary politics in Poland. Appeasement of the self-righteous imperial neighbor whose raw physical power is the sole foundation of its authority has been the dominant theme of every international and domestic policy. It is also the now publicly stated legitimacy of Communism. Even the official propaganda ceased to advance the ridiculous argument of the objective superiority of the Soviet system. But, it also is willing to point out that there can be no significant democratization of politics in Poland without a reduction of the Soviet hold over Eastern Europe. Such development is not likely to take place until an economic decline of the U.S.S.R. affects the Soviet military capabilities.

For as long as the post-World War II division of Europe continues, limited collaboration with the Communist authorities has no alternative for the majority of Poles. This had been a policy of the church and the ultimate test of patriotism, despite a heavy price involved by this attitude. It includes disruption of democratic-individualistic tradition and dislocation of economy by the characteristically Soviet lopsided development, with its heavy industry bias and irrational agricultural policy. Communist rule has also prolonged the almost two centuries old diaspora of the Polish nation. Since 1945, Poland has experienced several waves of immigration, that of 1980 involving over 100,000 citizens. Approximately fifteen million Poles, or one third of the entire nation, resides outside the country.

The price of Communism includes also a very painful decline of moral standards. The brutal and self-serving lawlessness of the authorities regarded as a foreign occupational power has provoked widespread corruption, quarrelsome aggressiveness, and a contemptuous attitude toward work. The nation became demoralized by an unscrupulous regime, with its deceptive propaganda and economic incompetence. Honesty and productive work have no value. The nation is also in a stage of internal immigration taking the form of withdrawal into private life, individual struggle for economic survival by entering subterreneal economy, and escape into alcoholism.

The situation in Poland today is that of waiting for something to happen. The Poles are fully aware of the pressing need for reforms, but they are checked by Soviet Russia. The government is too weak to pull Poland out of its socio-economic crisis contributing to a prevailing feeling of desperation. It is a dangerous situation, which may push impulsive and temper-mental Poles to uneven struggle with the U.S.S.R. The Soviets, perhaps, would welcome an excuse to crush Poland again as in 1830 and 1863, especially because out of four Soviet satellites in Central Europe only Poland avoided a second conquest. So far, Poland has not been overrun by the Soviet tanks like East Germany in 1953, Hungary in 1956 and Czechoslovakia in 1968. Soviet threat is only an abstraction to the young generation of Poles.

There is an alternative to another hopeless uprising followed by a Czechoslovak type of "normalization." The working class in Poland is searching for improved methods of non-violent resistance which would force the authorities to capitulate and give-up the monopoly of power, which they have not been able to exercise in a competent manner. It is a historical conflict patiently guided by the Roman Catholic church. After all, Christianity had prevailed over the first Rome, why not against the Third Rome. In any case, the events in Poland are only a preview to the struggle of the working class in Eastern Europe for emancipation from the arbitrary rule of Communism.

# Bibliography

"The Affair of the Deported Polish Leaders," Polish Fortnightly Review. London, May 15-June 1, 1945.

Anders, W. An Army in Exile. The Story of the Second Polish Corps. London: Macmillan and Co. Ltd., 1949.

Anders, Wladyslaw. Bez Ostatniego Rozdzialu, Wspomnienia z Lat 1939-1945. Newtown, 1950.

Anders, W. The Crime of Katyn. Facts and Documents. London: Polish Cultural Foundation, 1965.

Aron, Raymond. Peace and War. London: Weidenfield and Nicolson, 1966.

The Atlantic Community and Eastern Europe: Perspectives and Policy. The Atlantic Institute, July 1967.

Babinski, A. Witold. Przyczynki Historyczne od Okresu 1939-1945. Londyn: B. Swiderski, 1967.

Bajan, Konrad (ed). Podstawy Nauk Politycznych. Warszawa: Panstwowe Wydawnictwo Naukowe, 1972.

The Basic Law of the Federal Republic of Germany. New York: German Information Center, 1961.

Bauman, Zygmunt. "O Frustracji i o Kuglarzach," Kultura, No. 12/255 (1968).

Bauman, Zygmunt. "Twenty Years After: The Crisis of Soviet-Type Systems," Problems of Communism, No. 11-12, 1971.

Beck, Jozef. Final Report. New York: Robert Speller and Sons Publishers, Inc., 1957.

Benes, Vaclav L. and Pounds, Norman G. J. Poland. London: Ernest Benn Ltd., 1970.

Bethell, Nicholas. Gomulka: His Poland, His Communism. New York: Holt, Rinehart and Winston, 1969.

Bethell, Nicholas. The War Hitler Won. The Fall of Poland, September 1939. New York: Holt, Rinehart and Winston, 1972.

Birnbaum, Karl E. Peace in Europe. East-West Relations, 1966-1968 and the Prospects for a European Security. Oxford Paperbacks, 1970.

Borkowski, Jan. "Pertraktacje Przedwyborcze Miedzy Polska Partia Robotnicza i Polska Partia Socialistyczna a Polskim Stronnictwen Ludowym," Kwartalnik Historyczny, No. 2, 1964.

Bowie, Robert R. "A View from Poland," The Christian Science Monitor, May 29, 1974.

Bozyk, Pawel. RWPG, Ekonomiczny Mechanizm Wspolpracy. Ksiazka i Wiedza, 1970.

Brandt, Willy. In Exile. Essays, Reflections and Letters 1933-1947. London: Oswald Wolf, 1971.

Bregman, Aleksander. Zakamarki Historii. Londyn: Nakladem Polskiej Fundacji Kulturalnej, 1968.

Bromke, Adam. Poland's Politics; Idealism vs. Realism. Cambridge, Massachusetts: Harvard University Press, 1967.

Bromke, Adam and Rakowska-Harmstone, Theresa (eds). The Communist States in Disarray, 1965-1971. Minneapolis: University of Minnesota Press, 1972.

Bromke, Adam. "The 'Znak' Group in Poland," East Europe, No. 2, 1962.

Brzezinski, Zbigniew K. Alternative to Partition. New York: McGraw-Hill Book Company, 1965.

Brzezinski, Zbigniew K. "How the Cold War was Played," Foreign Affairs, Vol. 51, No. 1, 1972.

Brzezinski, Zbigniew and Griffith, William E. "Peaceful Engagement in Eastern Europe," Foreign Affairs, Vol. 39, No. 4, 1962.

Brezinski, Zbigniew. The Soviet Bloc. Unity and Conflict. Cambridge, Massachusetts: Harvard University Press, 1971.

Bulletin des Presse und Informationsamtes der Bundesregierung 1958, No. 11.

Byrnes, James F. Speaking Frankly. New York: Harper and Brothers Publishers, 1947.

Carezy, Gaston de. "Gomulka and the Intellectuals," East Europe, Vol. 13, No. 12, 1964.

Carr, Edward Hallett. German-Soviet Relations Between the Two World Wars, 1919-1939. Baltimore: The Johns Hopkins Press, 1951.

Chinowski, Krzysztow and Stepniewska, Anna. "Handel Zagraniczny Polski w 1974 Roku," Zycie Gospodarcze, February 2, 1975.

Chmielewska, A. Europejskie Kraje Demokracji Ludowej, 1944-1948. Warszawa: Ksiazka i Wiedza, 1972.

Ciebich, Andrzej. Na Obcej Ziemi. Polskie Sily Zbrojne z Zagranica, 1939-1945. Londyn: Wydawnictwo Swiatowego Zwiazku Polakow z Zagranica, 1947.

Ciechanowski, Jan. Defeat in Victory. New York: Doubleday and Company, Inc., 1947.

Ciechanowski, Jan. Powstanie Warszwskie. Londyn: Odnowa, 1971.

82nd Congress, 2nd Session. House Report No. 2505. December 22, 1951.

Deutsch, Karl W., Schweigler, Gebhard L., and Echinger, Lewis J. "Foreign Policy of the German Federal Republic," in Roy C. Macridis (ed). Foreign Policy in World Politics. Englewood Cliffs, New Jersey: Prentice-Hall, Inc., 1972.

"Dla Bezpieczenstwa Europy i Pokoju Swiata," Sprawy Miedzynarodowe, No. 5, 1955.

Documents on Polish-Soviet Relations, 1939-1945, Vols. I & II. London: Heinemann, General Sikorski Institute, 1961.

Dobrska, Z., and Hirszowa, A. Plan Schumana. Narzedzie Imperialistycznej Agresji Stanow Zjednoczonych Ameryki Polnocnej w Europie. Warsaw: Panstwowy Instytut Spraw Miedzynarodowych, 1950.

Djornik, Francis. The Making of Central and Eastern Europe. London: The Polish Research Centre, Ltd., 1949.

"European Security System: Content and Ways of Ensuring It," International Affairs. Moscow, November 1971.

Feldman, Wilhelm. Dzieje Polskiej Mysli Politicznej. Warszawa, 1933.

Fleming, George J. "The Polish Eagle Looks West," East Europe, No. 10, 1967.

Foreign Relations of the United States. Diplomatic Papers. The Conference at Malta and Yalta 1945. Washington, D.C.: United States Government Printing Office, 1955.

"Freedom Maifesto of 34 Polish Intellectuals," in Tadeusz N. Cieplak (ed). Poland Since 1956. New York: Twayne Publishers, Inc., 1972.

140

Frelek, Ryszard. "Wielostronna Sila Nuklearna NATO," Sprawy Miedzynarodowe, No. 1, 1964.

Gajda, Eugeniusz. Polska Polityka Zagraniczna, 1944-1974. Warszawa: Ministerstwo Obrony Narodowej, 1974.

Gamarnikow, Michael. "Another Step Toward Private Enterprise," East Europe, Vol. 17, No. 1, 1968.

Gamarnikow, Michael. "Poland's Economic Recession," East Europe, Vol. 12, No. 3, 1963.

Gamarnikow, Michael. "Polityka Gospodarcza Gierka," Na Antenie, No. 111, 1972.

Gati, Charles. "The Forgotten Region," Foreign Policy, No. 19, 1975.

German Polish Dialogue.Letters of the Polish and German Bishops and International Statements. New York: Atlantic Forum, 1966.

Germany and Eastern Europe since 1945. From the Potsdam Agreement to Chancellor Brandt's "Ostpolitik." New York: Charles Scribner's Sons, 1973.

Gierek, Edward. "Przemowienie na VIII Plenum KC PZPR," in Stanislaw Machete (ed). Podstawy Nauk Politycznych, Vol. I. Warszawa: Ksiazka i Wiedza, 1972.

Giertych, Jedrzej. Politika Polska w Dziejach Europy. Londyn: Nakladem Autora, 1947.

Gieysztor, Aleksander (ed). History of Poland. Warsaw: Polish Scientific Publishers, 1968

Glowczyk, Jan and Misiak, Marek. "The Future of the Economy," Polish Perspectives, No. 10, 1968.

Gomulka, Wl. (Wieslaw) and Minc, Hilary. Nasza Gospodarka na Ziemiach Odzyskanych. Ksiazka, Wiedza, 1946.

Gomulka, Wladyslaw (Wieslaw). Oboz Demoktratyczny Buduje Polske z Woli Narodu. Warszawa: Spoldzielnia Wydawnicza Ksiazka, 1946.

Gomulka, Wladyslaw. "Writers and Socialism," in Tadeusz N. Cieplak (ed). Poland Since 1956. New York: Twayne Publishers, Inc., 1972.

Gomulka, Wladyslaw. "Znaczenie Miedzynarodowych Ukladow z CSRS, NRD i Bulgaria oraz Konferencji w Karlowych Warach," Nowe Drogi, No. 5, 1967.

141

Gomulka, Wladyslaw (Wieslaw). "I Zjazd Polskiej Partii Robotnizej," in Ku Nowej Polsce. Spoldzielnia Wydawnicza "Ksiazka," 1945.

Gora, Stanislaw and Krzyziak, Zygmunt. Miedzynarodowa Specjalizacja Produkcji Krajow RWPG. Warszawa: Panstwowe Wydawnictwo Gospodarcze, 1974.

Gorcgey, Laszlo. "Emerging Patterns in West Germany-East Europe Relations," ORBIS, No. 3, 1966.

Groth, Alexander J. People's Poland: Government and Politics. London: Chandler Publishing Company, 1972.

Gruchman, Bohdan, and others. Polish Western Territories. Poznan: Instytut Zachodni, 1959.

Grunberg, Karol. Historia Polski w Latach 1939-1947. Torun, 1971.

Halecki, Oscar. Borderlands of Western Civilization. A History of East Central Europe. New York: The Ronald Press Company, 1952.

Halecki, Oscar. A History of Poland. New York: Roy Publishers, 1956.

Hamilton, Hamish. The Goebbels Diaries. London, 1948.

Hanrieder, Wolfram F. The Stable Crisis. New York: Harper and Row Publishers, 1970.

Hanrieder, Wolfram F. West German Foreign Policy, 1949-1963. Stanford, California: Stanford University Press, 1967.

Hassner, Pierre. "Change and Security in Europe. Part II: In Search of a System," Adelphi Papers, No. 49, 1968.

Hauptmann, Jerzy. "Hopes and Fears of German Reunification: A Polish View" in David S. Collier and Kurt Glaser (eds). Western Policy and Eastern Europe. Chicago: Henry Regney Company, 1966.

Hiscocks, Richard. Poland. Bridge for the Abyss? London: Oxford University Press, 1963.

Hoffmann, Michal. "O Niemcy Pokojowe, Demokratyczne i Zjednoczone," Nowe Drogi, No. 4, 1952.

Horak, Stephen (ed). Poland's International Affairs, 1919-1960. Bloomington: Indiana University Press, 1964.

"Hugh Gibson Compares the Poland of 1919 with that of 1946," Polish Review, November 28, 1946.

142

Ireland, Brian. "Poland" in R. R. Betts (ed). Central and South East Europe. London: Royal Institute of International Affairs, 1950.

Jacobsen, Hans-Adolf and Tomala, Mieczyslaw (eds). Wie Polen und Deutsche Einander Sehen. Dusseldorf: Droste Verlag, 1973.

Jaksch, Wenzel. Europe's Road to Potsdam. New York: Frederich A. Praeger, 1963.

Jamgotch, Nish Jr. Soviet-East European Dialogue. International Relations of a New Type? Stanford: Stanford University, The Hoover Institution on War, Revolution and Peace, 1968.

Janicki, Andrzej. "Chiny a Europa," Perspektywy, February 7, 1975.

Jaroszewicz, Piotr. "Zalozenia Rozwoju Gospodarczego Kraju w Latach 1971-1975," in Stanislaw Machete (ed). Podstawy Nauk Politycznych, Vol. I. Warszawa: Ksiazka i Wiedza, 1972.

Kakol, Jozef. The Logic of the Oder-Neisse Frontier. Poznan: Wydawnictwo Zachodnie, 1959.

Kartesz, Stephen D. (ed). East Central Europe and the World: Developments in the Post-Stalin Era. University of Notre Dame Press, 1962.

Keef, Eugene K. and others, Area Handbook for Poland. Washington, D.C.: U.S. Government Printing Office, 1973.

Khrushchev Remembers. The Last Testament. Boston: Little, Brown and Company, 1974.

Kielczewska-Zalewska, Maria. "The Geographic Basis of Poland," in Zygmund Wojciechowski (ed). Poland's Place in Europe. Poznan: Instytut Zachodni, 1947.

Kintner, William R. and Klaiber, Wolfgang. Eastern Europe and European Security. New York: Dunellen, 1971.

Klafkowski, Alfons. "Uklad Polska-NRF o Podstwawach Normalizacji Stosunkow jako Element Uznania status quo w Europie," Sprawy Miedzynarodowe, No. 9, 1971.

Klafkowski, Alfons. Umowa Poczdamska a Sprawy Polskie, 1945-1970. Poznan: Wydawnictwo Poznanskie, 1970.

Klimkowski, J. Bylem Adiutantem Gen Andersa. Warszawa: MON, 1959.

Kolakowski, Leszek. "Permanent and Transitory Aspects of Marxism," in Pawel Maxewski (ed). The Broken Mirror. New York: Random House, 1958.

Konovalev, S. Russo-Polish Relations. A Historical Survey. Princeton, New Jersey: Princeton University Press, 1945.

Korbel, Josef. "West Germany's Ostpolitik: A Policy Toward the Soviet Allies," ORBIS, No. 14, Summer 1971.

Kot, Stanislaw. Conversations with the Kremlin and Dispatches from Russia. London: Oxford University Press, 1963.

Kowalski, Wlodzimierz T. Polityka Zagraniczna RP, 1944-1947. Warszawa: Polski Instytut Spraw Miedzynarodowych, 1971.

Kowalski, Wlodzimierz T. Walka Dyplomatyczna o Miejsce Polski w Europie. Warszawa: Ksiazka i Wiedza, 1972.

Kozinski, Stanislaw. "Consumption and the Market," Polish Perspectives, No. 3, 1968.

Kozlowski, Eligiusz and Wrzosek, Mieczyslaw. Dzieje Oreza Polskiego 1974-1938. Warszawa: Wydawnictwo Ministerstwa Obrony Narodoweji, 1973.

Krasicki, Ignacy. "Status quo i Bezpieczenstwo Europejskie," Sprawy Miedzynarodowe, No. 11, 1968.

Krasuski, Jerzy. Historia Rzeszy Niemiedziej 1871-1945. Wydawnictwo Poznanskie, 1969.

Krzesinski, Andrew J. Poland's Rights to Justice. New York: The Devin-Adair Company, 1946.

Kulczynski, Leon. "Granice Uprzejmosei Kurta-Georga Kiesingera," Nowe Drogi, No. 4, 1967.

Kulski, W. W. "Central Europe in Transition," Journal of Central European Affairs, No. 4, 1949.

Kukiel, Marian. General Sikorski. London: Instytut Polski i Muzem im. Gen. Sikorskiego, 1970.

Kuron, Jacek and Modzelewski, Karol. "An Open Letter to the Party" in Julius Jacobson (ed). Soviet Communism and the Socialist Vision. New Brunswick, New Jersey: Transaction Books, 1972.

Kusmierz, Bronislaw. Stalin and the Poles. London: Hollis and Carter, 1949.

144

Labedz, Leo. "Detente or Deception," East-West Digest, No. 16, August 1974.

Lachs, Manfred. "Konferencja Warszawska," Nowe Drogi, No. 5, 1955.

Laguewo, Walter. The Rebirth of Europe. New York: Holt, Rinehart and Winston, 1970.

Lampe, Alfred. Miejsce Polski w Europie. Moskwa: Nakladem Zwiazku Partiotow Polskich w ZSRR, 1944.

Lane, Arthur Bliss. I Saw Poland Betrayed. New York: The Bobbs-Merrill Company, 1948.

Lange, Oskar. Dwie Drogi Rozwoju w Gospodace Swiatowej. Warszawa: Panstwowy Instytut Spraw Miedzynaradowych, 1950.

Lange, Oskar. "Poland's Foreign Policy," Poland of Today, March 1946.

Lange, Oskar. "Rola Polski w Powojennym Swiecie," in Na Progu Wolnosci. London: Polish Progressive Club, 1944.

Larski, Wiktor. "Plan Schumana-Narzedzie Imperialstycznej Agresji," Sprawy Miedzynarodowe, Vol. 6, 1952.

Larski, Witold. "Uklad o Bezpiecznstwie Zbiorowym w Europie," Sprawy Miedzynarodowe, No. 2, 1954.

Lednicki, Waclaw. Life and Culture of Poland. New York: Roy Publishers, 1944.

Lenin, V. I. On the National Question and Proletarian Internationalism. Moscow: Novosti Press Agency Publishing House, 1969.

Leslie, R. F. The Polish Question: Poland's Place in Modern History. London: The Historical Association, 1964.

Lesniewski, Andrzej (ed). Western Frontier of Poland. Warsaw: Polish Intitute of International Affairs, 1965.

The Liquidation of Poland, Voluntary or Compulsory? And by Whose Authority? Glasgow: P. Donegan and Co., Ltd., 1945.

Litauer, Stefan. Zmierzch "Londynu." Warszawa: Spoldzielnia Wydawnicza "Czytelnik," 1945.

London, Jurt L. "Eastern Europe in the Communist World," in Robert F. Byrnes (ed). The United States and Eastern Europe. Englewood Cliffs, New Jersey: Prentice-Hall, Inc., 1967.

Lowis, Flora. A Case History of Hope. The Story of Poland's Peaceful Revolution. New York: Doubleday and Company, Inc., 1958.

Lukasiewicz, Juliusz. Polska jest Mocarstwem. Warszawa: Gubethner and Wolff, 1939.

Markiewicz, Ryszard. "Polska, NRD i Bezpieczenstwo Europy," Sprawy Miedzynarodowe, No. 4, 1967.

Merkl, Peter H. German Foreign Policies, West and East. Santa Barbara, California: American Bibliographical Center--Clio Press, Inc., 1974.

Mikolajczyk, Stanislaw. "The Polish Government and the Future of Poland," Polish Review, September 13, 1944.

Mikolajczyk, Stanislaw. The Rape of Poland. New York: McGraw-Hill Book Company, Inc., 1948.

"Moscow Talks and Trials," Free Europe, June 29, 1945.

"Nauki Wydarzen," Kultura, No. 6/248-7/249, 1968.

Nowak, Jan. "The Church in Poland," Problems of Communism, January-February, 1982.

Nowak, Jan. "Conflict of Generations in Poland," East Europe, No. 5, 1968.

Nowak, Jan. "The Struggle for Party Control," East Europe, No. 5, 1968.

Nowak, Jan. "W Poszukiwaniu Trzeciej Drogi," Na Antenie, No. 95, 1971.

Oakes, John B. The Edge of Freedom. New York: Harper and Brothers Publishers, 1961, Chapter 13.

Olszowski, Stefan. "Polish Foreign Policy in the Age of Detente." Polish Perspectives, No. 3, 1974.

Opolski, A.K. A Nation in Fetters. Newtown: Montgomeryshire Printing Company, Ltd., 1947.

Osborne, R. H. East-Central Europe. An Introductory Geography. New York: Frederich A. Praeger Company, 1967.

Osobka-Morawski, Edward. Materialy do Historii Polski. Unpublished.

Osobka-Morawski, Edward and Gomulka, Wl. (Wieslaw). Narod Chce Spokoju i Przepedzi Precz Podzegaczy do Walk Bratobojczych. Katowice: Wydawnictwo Trybuny Robotniczej, March 1946.

146

Palmer, Alan. The Lands Between a History of East-Central Europe Since the Congress of Vienna. New York: The Macmillan Company, 1970.

Pekalski, Jerzy. "Struktura Obrotow Polsko-Radzieckich," Zycie Gospodarcze, January 26, 1975.

Piorkowski, Jerzy. "Ghost or Man?" Poland, April 1968.

Piorkowski, Jerzy. "Suwerennosc Rzecz Realna i Znana," Nowe Drogi, Nos. 11-12, 1956.

"Po Wizycie de Gaulle'a--Proba Bilansu," Sprawy Miedzynarodowe, No. 10, 1967.

Pobog-Maliniwski, Wladyslaw. Najnowsza Historia Polityczna Polski, 1914-1939, Vol. III. London: B. Swiderski, 1967.

Podkowinski, Marian. "Olbrzym Czy Karzel?" Perspektywy, January, 1975.

Podkowinski, Marian. "Wymowne Milczenie," Perspektywy, March 21, 1975.

Podstawy Nauk Politicznych, Dokumenty i Materialy, Vol. I, 2nd edition. Warszawa: Ksiazka i Wiedza, 1972.

Polaczek, Stanislaw. Integracja Gospodarcza Krajow Socjalistycznych a Handel Zagraniczny Polski. Warszawa: Panstwowe Wydawnictwo Ekonomiczne, 1971.

"Poles, East Germany Bury the Hatchet," The Christian Science Monitor, June 26, 1974.

The Polish Election, 19th January, 1947. London: British Joint Committee for Polish Affairs, 1947.

"Polish Foreign Policy: A Chronology," Polish Perspectives, No. 4, 1974.

"Polityka Zagraniczna Polski Ludowej," Sprawy Miedzynarodowe, No. 4, 1952.

Polska Ludowa-Zwiazek Radziecki, 1944-1974. Zbior Dokumentow i Materialow. Warszawa: Ministerstwo Spraw Zagranicznych Polskiej Rzeczypospolitej Ludowe and Ministerstwo Spraw Zagranicznych Zwiazku Socjalistycznych Republik Radzieckich, 1974.

"Polski Pazdziernik," Po Prostu, October 28, 1956.

Posen-Zawadzki, K. "Z Dziejow Powstania i Ewakuacji Wojska Polskiego z ZSRR," Wojskowy Przeglad Historyczny, No. 2, 1963.

Pounds, Norman J. G. Poland Between East and West. Princeton, New Jersey: D. Van Nostrand Company, Inc., 1964.

Ptakowski, Jerzy. "Gomulka and His Party," East Europe, No. 5, 1967.

"The Polish Government Memorandum Concerning the Creation of an Atom-Free Zone in Central Europe," in Polish Viewpoint, Disarmament, Denuclearization, European Security, Documents, Declarations, Statements. Warsaw: "Polania" Publishing House, 1967.

Prittie, Tarance. Konrad Adenauer, 1876-1967. London: Tom Stacey, 1972.

Ptakowski, Jerzy. "The Fifth Polish Party Congress," East Europe, No. 1, 1969.

Puacz, Edward. "Przeslanki Nowej Mysli Politycznej," in Na Progu Wolnosci. London: Polish Progressive Club, 1944.

Puacz, Edward. "Sprawa Granic Polski w Ukladach Miedzy PKWN i ZSRR," Kultura, Zeszyty Historyczne, 15. Paryz: Instytut Literacki, 1969.

"The Fate of Polish Socialism" Foreign Affairs, No. 1, October, 1949.

Rakowski, Mieczyslaw. "A Year Later," Polish Perspectives, No. 2, 1972.

"Resolution of the Polish Writers the City of Warsaw Branch," in Tadeusz N. Cieplak (ed). Poland Since 1956. New York: Twayne Publishers, Inc., 1972.

"Rewolucja Palacowa," Na Antenie, No. 95, 1971.

Rhode, Gotthold and Wagner, Wolfgang (eds). The Genesis of the Oder-Neisse Line. Stuttgart: Brentano-Verlag, 1959.

Roberts, Henry L. Eastern Europe: Politics, Revolution and Diplomacy. New York: Alfred A. Knopf, 1970.

Rocznik Statystyczny, 1974.Warszawa: Glowny Urzad Statystyczny, 1956-1974.

Roos, Hans. A History of Modern Poland. London: Eyre and Spottiswoode, 1966.

148

Rotfeld, Adam Daniel and Skowronski, Andrzej. "Polska, Niemcy i Bezpieczenstwo Europy," Sprawy Miedzynarodowe, Nos. 7-8, 1968.

Rozek, Edward J. Wartime Diplomacy. A Pattern in Poland. London: John Wiley and Sons, Inc., 1958.

Rurarz, Zdzislaw M. Polish Foreign Trade. Warszawa: Ksiazka i Wiedza, 1969.

Rzendowski, Ignacy. "Handel Zagraniczny USA a Plan Marshala," Nowe Drogi, No. 9, 1948.

Schmitt, F. J. (ed). Im Deutschen Bundestag, Deutschland und Ostpolitik 1. Bonn: Pfattheicher and Reichardt, 1973.

Schub, Anatole. "Lessons from Czechsolovakia," Foreign Affairs, No. 2, 1969.

Schwoebel, Jean. "La champion de la securite collective en Europe," Le Monde Diplomatique, May 1974.

Seabury, Paul. The Rise and Decline of the Cold War. New York: Basic Books, Inc., 1967.

Sharp, Samuel L. Poland. White Eagle on a Red Field. Cambridge, Massachusetts: Harvard University Press, 1953.

Shotwell, James T. and Laserson, Max M. Poland and Russia 1919-1945. New York: King's Crown Press, 1945.

Siemiaszko, Z. S. "Powstanie Warszawskie--Kontakty ZSRR i PKWN," Kultura, Zeszyty Historyczne, 16. Paryz: Instytut Literacki, 1969.

Sikora, Jozef. "Tradycje Zdrady i Tradycje Patriotyzmu," Nowe Drogi, No. 47, 1953.

Skilling, H. Gordon. The Government of Communist East Europe. New York: Thomas Y. Crowell Company, 1971.

Skolimowski, Henryk. "Leszek Kolakowski--Fenomen Polskiego Marksizmu," Kultura, No. 5/261, 1969.

Skowronski, Andrzej. Polska a Problem Niemic, 1945-1965. Warszawa: Panstwowy Instytut Spraw Miedzynarodowych, Ksiazka i Wiedza, 1967.

Skowronski, Andrzej. "Problemy Bezpieczenstwa Zbiorowego w Europie," Sprawy Miedzynarodowe, No. 7-8, 1965.

Sobezak, Janusz. "Polityka Wschodnia SPD (Part II)," Sprawy Miedzynarodowe, No. 2, 1969.

"Speech by Wladyslaw Gomulka," Polish Perspectives, No. 4, 1968.

Staar, Richard F. Poland 1944-1962. The Sovietization of a Captive People. New Orleans: Louisiana State University Press, 1962.

Stanislawska, Stefania. Polska a Monachium. Warszawa: Ksiazka i Wiedza, 1967.

Steele, Jonathan (ed). Eastern Europe Since Stalin. New York: Crane, Russak and Company, Inc., 1974.

Stehle, Hansjakob. The Independent Satellite. London: Fredrick A. Praeger, 1965.

Stern, Peter H. The Struggle for Poland. Washington, D.C.: Public Affairs Press, 1953.

Su-Cardwell, Ann. The Case for Poland. Ann Arbor, Michigan, 1945.

Sulek, Jerzy. "Organizacje Przesiedlencze a 'Nowa Polityka Wschodnia NRF,'" Sprawy Miedzynarodowe, No. 6, 1968.

Swiatlo, Jozef. Za Kulisami Bezpieki i Partii. No publisher, 1954.

Sworakowski, Witold. "An Error Regarding Eastern Galicia in Curzon's Note to the Soviet Government," Journal of Central European Affairs, No. 1, 1944.

"Symbole i Konkrety," Zycie Gospodarcze, November 10, 1974.

Szaz, Zoltan M. Germany's Eastern Frontiers. Chicago: Henry Regnery Company, 1960.

Szczepanski, Jan. "The Polish Intelligentsia. Past and Present," in Tadeusz N. Cieplak (ed). Poland Since 1956. New York: Twayne Publishers, Inc., 1972.

Szenfeld, Ignacy. "The Reminiscences of Wladislaw Gomulka," Radio Liberty, 1975.

Szymanski, Zygmunt. "O Filizofi Politycznej de Gaulle'a," Sprawy Miedzynarodowe, No. 6, 1967.

Szyndler-Glowacki, Wieslaw. "Jak Dalej Handlowac z Amerykanami?" Zycie Gospodarcze, October 6, 1974.

Tarnowski, Adam. Two Polish Attempts to Bring about a Central-East European Organization. Lecture delivered in London, October, 1943.

150

Tomala, Mieczyslaw. "Glowne Kierunka Polityki Zagranicznej Rzadu NRF," Sprawy Miedzynaradowe, No. 12, 1967.

Tomala, Mieczyslaw (ed). Walka o Jednosc Niemiec. Dokumenty Materialy. Warsaw, 1953.

Towpik, Andrzej. "O Ogolndeuropejskim Systemie Bezpieczenstwa," Sprawy Miedzynaradowe, No. 1, 1972.

The Treaty Between the Federal Republic of Germany and the People's Republic of Poland. Press and Information Office of the Federal Govermnent, 1971.

Triska, Jan F. (ed). Constitutions of the Communist Party-States. Stanford, California: The Hoover Institution on War, Revolution and Peace, Stanford University, 1968.

Troscianko, Wiktor. "Polish Journalists and the Censor," East Europe, No. 11, 1965.

Trotter, Bernard and Watson, J. W. "Poland in the European Balance," Canadian Geographical Journal, No. 29, September, 1944.

Turlejska, Maria. Rok Przed Kleska. 1 Wrzesnia 1938-1 Wrzesnia 1939. Warszawa: Powszechna Wiedza, 1969.

Ulam, Adam B. Expansionism and Coexistence. The History of Soviet Foreign Policy 1917-1967. New York: Frederich A. Praeger, 1968.

Valkener, Elizabeth K. "The Catholic Church in Poland, 1945-1955," Review of Politics, No. 3, 1956.

Vierheller, Viktoria. Polen und die Deutschland-Frage 1939-1949. Koln: Verlag Wissenschaft und Politik, 1970.

Vaughan, Michalina. "A Multidimensional Approach to Contemporary Polish Stratification," Survey, No. 1, 1974.

Walczek, Antoni Wladyslaw. BHE, Zachodnioniemiecka Partia Przesiedlenclow. Poznan: Instytut Zachodni, 1966.

Wandycz, Piotr S. Czechoslovak-Polish Confederation and the Great Powers 1940-43. Indiana University Publications, Slavic and East European Series, Vol. 3, 1956.

Wandycz, Piotr S. Soviet-Polish Relations, 1917-1921. Cambridge, Massachusetts: Harvard University Press, 1968.

Wawczuk, Wlodzimierz. "Instrument Przyspieszenia," Perspektywy, April 4, 1975.

151

Weinberg, Gerhard L. The Foreign Policy of Hitler's Germany. Diplomatic Revolt in Europe, 1933-36. Chicago: The University of Chicago Press, 1970.

Weit, Erwin. At the Red Summit. New York: Macmillan Publishing Co., Inc., 1973.

Werfel, Roman. "Przeciw Nacjonalizmowi i Kosmopolityzmowi," Nowe Drogi, Nos. 5-6, 1949.

Whetten, Lawrance L. Germany's Ostpolitik; Relations Between the Federal Republic and the Warsaw Pact Countries. London: Oxford University Press, 1971.

White, Peter T. "Springtime of Hope in Poland," National Geographic, Vol. 141, April 1972.

Wieczorek, Wlodzimierz. "Historyczny Rozwoj Idei Bezpieczenstwa Europejskiego," Sprawy Miedzynaradowe, No. 9, 1970.

Wiejacz, Jozef. "Nowy Etap Tworzenia Trwatego Bezpieczenstwa w Europie," Sprawy Miedzynarodowe, Nos. 7-8, 1973.

Wighton, Charles. Adenauer-Democratic Dictator. London: Frederick Muller Ltd., 1963.

Williams, T. Harry, Current, Richard N., and Freidel, Frank. A History of the United States. New York: Alfred A. Knopf, 1969.

Wilpert, Friedrich von. The Oder-Neisse Problem. New York: Atlantic-Forum, 1969.

Windsor, Philip. Germany and the Management of Detente. London: Chatto and Windus, 1971.

Winiewicz, Jozef. "A New Chapter," Polish Perspectives, No. 2, 1971.

Winiewicz, Jozef. "Poland and the German Problem," Poland of Today, January 1948.

Winiewicz, Jozef. "Speech at the U.N. General Assembly." October 10, 1966, in Polish Viewpoint. Disarmament, Denuclearization, European Security, Documents, Declarations, Statements. Warsaw: "Polonia" Publishing House, 1967.

Wojciechowski, Zygmund. "Poland and Germany, Ten Centuries of Struggle," in Zygmund Wojciechowski (ed). Poland's Place in Europe. Poznan: Instytut Zachodni, 1947.

Woods, William. Poland: Eagle in the East. New York: Hill and Wang, 1968.

152

VI Zjazd Polskiej Zjednoczonej Partii Robotniczej, 6-11 December
    1971, Podstawowe Materialy i Dokumenty.  Warsaw, 1972.

Zawodny, J. K.  Nothing But Honour.  Stanford:  Hoover
    Institution Press, 1978.

# Index of Personal Names

Rapacki, Adam 21-22,
   24-25, 27, 101
Rokossowsky, Konstanty
   18-19, 91-92, 95
Roosevelt, Franklin D. 57
Rzymowski, W. 61

Schumacher, Kurt 67
Sikorski, Wladyslaw 3-4,
   6, 52-55, 86
Spychalski, Marian 110
Stalin, Joseph 7, 13-15,
   54-55, 64, 86
Strauss, Franz-Joseph 43,
   71

Truman, Harry S. 62

Ulbricht, Walter 38, 66,
   72, 112, 121

Walesa, Lech 126
Wyszynski, Stefan
   Cardinal 103-104, 118,
   135